Business Analytics

Business Analytics

A Data-Driven Decision Making Approach for Business

Volume I

Amar Sahay, PhD

BEP BUSINESS EXPERT PRESS

Business Analytics: A Data-Driven Decision Making Approach for Business, Volume I

First published in 2018 by
Business Expert Press, LLC
222 East 46th Street, New York, NY 10017
www.businessexpertpress.com

ISBN-13: 978-1-63157-331-6 (paperback)
ISBN-13: 978-1-63157-332-3 (e-book)

Business Expert Press Big Data and Business Analytics Collection

Collection ISSN: 2333-6749 (print)
Collection ISSN: 2333-6757 (electronic)

Cover and interior design by Exeter Premedia Services Private Ltd., Chennai, India

First edition: 2018

10 9 8 7 6 5 4 3 2 1

Printed in the United States of America.

Abstract

This book is about Business Analytics (BA)—an emerging area in modern business decision making. The first part provides an overview of the field of Business Intelligence (BI) that looks into historical data to better understand business performance thereby improving performance, and creating new strategic opportunities for growth. Business analytics (BA) is about anticipated future trends of the key performance indicators used to automate and optimize business processes. The three major categories of business analytics—the *descriptive, predictive,* and *prescriptive* analytics along with advanced analytics tools are explained. The flow diagrams outlining the tools of each of the descriptive, predictive, and prescriptive analytics are presented. We also describe a number of terms related to business analytics.

The second part of the book is about *descriptive analytics* and its applications. The topics discussed are—Data, Data Types and Descriptive Statistics, Data Visualization, Data Visualization with Big Data, Basic Analytics Tools: Describing Data Numerically—Concepts and Computer Applications. Finally, an overview and a case on descriptive statistics with applications and notes on implementation are presented. The concluding remarks provide information on becoming a certified analytics professional (CAP) and an overview of the second volume of this book which is a continuation of this first volume. It is about predictive analytics which is the application of predictive models to predict future trends. The second volume discusses *Prerequisites for Predictive Modeling; Most Widely used Predictive Analytics Models, Linear and Non-linear regression, Forecasting Techniques, Data mining, Simulation, and Data Mining.*

Keywords

analytics, business analytics, business intelligence, data analysis, data mining, decision making, descriptive analytics, machine learning, modeling, neural networks, optimization, predictive analytics, predictive modeling, prescriptive analytics, quantitative techniques, regression analysis, simulation, statistical analysis, time-series forecasting

Contents

Preface ix

Acknowledgments xv

Part I **Foundations of Business Analytics (BA)** 1

Chapter 1 Business Analytics (BA) at a Glance 3

Chapter 2 Business Intelligence (BI), Business Analytics (BA),
and Data Analytics 29

Part II **Descriptive Analytics** 57

Chapter 3 Data, Data Types, and Descriptive Statistics 59

Chapter 4 Descriptive Analytics: Data Visualization 79

Chapter 5 Data Visualization with Big Data 125

Chapter 6 Basic Analytics Tools: Describing Data
Numerically—Concepts and Computer Analysis 139

Chapter 7 Wrap-up, Cases, and Notes on Implementation 195

References 215

Additional Readings 217

About the Author 219

Index 221

Preface

This book deals with business analytics (BA)—an emerging area in modern business decision making.

BA is a data driven decision making approach that uses statistical and quantitative analysis, information technology, management science (mathematical modeling, simulation), along with data mining and fact-based data to measure past business performance to guide an organization in business planning, predicting the future outcomes, and effective decision making.

BA tools are also used to visualize and explore the patterns and trends in the data to predict future business outcomes with the help of forecasting and predictive modeling.

In this age of technology, companies collect massive amount of data. Successful companies use their data as an asset and use them for competitive advantage. These companies use BA tools as an organizational commitment to data-driven decision making. BA helps businesses in making informed business decisions. It is also critical in automating and optimizing business processes.

BA makes extensive use of data, statistical analysis, mathematical and statistical modeling, and data mining to explore, investigate and understand the business performance. Through data, BA helps to gain insight and drive business planning and decisions. The tools of BA focus on understanding business performance based on the data and a number of models derived from statistics, management science, and operations research areas.

The BA area can be divided into different categories depending upon the types of analytics and tools being used. The major categories of BA are:

- Descriptive analytics
- Predictive analytics
- Prescriptive analytics

Each of the previously mentioned categories uses different tools and the use of these analytics depends on the type of business and the operations a company is involved in. For example, an organization may only use descriptive analytics tools; whereas another company may use a combination of descriptive and predictive modeling and analytics to predict future business performance to drive business decisions.

The different types of analytics and the tools used in these analytics are described as follows:

1. **Descriptive analytics**: Involves the use of descriptive statistics including the graphical and numerical methods to describe the data. Successful use and implementation of descriptive analytics requires the understanding of types of data, graphical/visual representation of data, and graphical techniques using computer. The other aspect of descriptive analytics is an understanding of numerical methods including the measures of central tendency, measures of position, measures of variation, and measures of shape, and how different measures and statistics are used to summarize and draw conclusions from the data. Some other topics of interest are the understanding of empirical rule and the relationship between two variables—the covariance, and correlation coefficient. The tools of descriptive analytics are helpful in understanding the data, identifying the trend or patterns in the data, and making sense from the data contained in the databases of companies. The understanding of databases, data warehouse, web search and query, and Big Data concepts are important in extracting and applying descriptive analytics tools.

   Besides the descriptive statistics tools described earlier, an understanding of a number of other descriptive analytics tools is critical in describing and drawing meaningful conclusion from the data. These include: (a) Probability theory and its role in decision making, (b) Sampling and inference procedures, (c) Estimation and confidence intervals, (d) Hypothesis testing/inference procedures for one and two population parameters, and (e) Chi-square and nonparametric tests. The understanding of these tools is critical in understanding and applying inferential statistics tools—a critical part of data analysis and decision making.

2. ***Predictive analytics***: As the name suggests predictive analytics is the application of predictive models that are used to predict future trends. The most widely used models are regression and forecasting models. Variations of regression models include: (a) Simple regression models, (b) Multiple regression models, (c) Non-linear regression models including the quadratic or second-order models, and polynomial regression models, (d) Regression models with indicator or qualitative independent variables, and (e) Regression models with interaction terms or interaction models. Regression models are one of the most widely used models in various types of applications. These models are used to explain the relationship between a response variable and one or more independent variables. The relationship may be linear or curvilinear. The objective of these regression models is to predict the response variable using one or more independent variables or predictors.

The predictive models also involve a class of time series analysis and forecasting models. The commonly used forecasting models are regression-based models that use regression analysis to forecast future trend. Other time series forecasting models are simple moving average, moving average with trend, exponential smoothing, exponential smoothing with trend, and forecasting seasonal data. All these predictive models are used to forecast the future trend.

Other Models and Tools Used in Predictive Modeling

Data mining, machine learning, and neural network applications are also integral part of predictive analytics. The following topics are introduced in this text.

Data Mining and Advanced Data Analysis
    Definition of Machine Learning and related terms
    Online Analytical Processing (OLAP)
    Data Visualization and Software for Data Visualization
Data Classification Methods and Introduction to
    Logistic Regression
    Machine Learning
    Neural Networks
    Classification and Clustering

3. *Prescriptive analytics*: Prescriptive analytics is concerned with optimal allocation of resources in an organization. A number of operations research and management science tools have been applied for allocating the limited resources in the most effective way. The operations management tools are derived from management science, industrial engineering including the simulation tools which are also used to study different types of manufacturing and service organizations. These are proven tools and techniques in studying and understanding the operations and processes of organizations. The tools of operations management can be divided into mainly three areas. These are (a) planning, (b) analysis, and (c) control tools. The analysis part is the prescriptive analysis part that uses the operations research, management science, and simulation tools. The control part is used to monitor and control the product and service quality. There are a number of prescriptive analytics tool in use today. The following are some of the prescriptive analytics models:

(1) Linear optimization models including maximization and minimization of different resources—involves computer analysis and sensitivity analysis
(2) Integer linear optimization models
(3) Nonlinear optimization models
(4) Simulation modeling and applications areas
(5) Monte Carlo simulation
    Simulations using Excel, @Risk, Crystal Ball
    Simulation using ProModel:
(6) Analysis of variance and design of experiments

The aforementioned analytics tools come under the broad area of *Business Intelligence (BI)* that incorporates *Business Analytics (BA), Data Analytics, and Advanced Analytics*. All these areas come under the umbrella of business intelligence (BI) and use a number of visual and mathematical *models*.

Modeling is one the most important part of BA. Models are of different types. An understanding of different types of models is critical in selecting and applying the right model or models to solve business problems.

Among the models and related details described are: (a) Graphical models, (b) Quantitative models, (c) Algebraic models, (d) Spreadsheet models, and (e) Other analytic tools.

Most of the tools in descriptive, predictive, and prescriptive analytics are described using one or the other type of model, which are mathematical and computer models. Besides these models, simulation and a number of other mathematical models are used in analytics.

BA is a vast area. It is not possible to provide a complete and in-depth treatment of the BA topics in one concise book; therefore, the book is divided into following two parts:

- *Business Analytics: A Data Driven Decision Making Approach for Business—Part I*
- *Business Analytics: A Data Driven Decision Making Approach for Business—Part II*

The first volume of the book discusses BA, BI, data analytics and the role and importance of these in the modern business decision making. It outlines and discusses the different areas of BA: (1) Descriptive analytics, (2) Predictive analytics, and (3) Prescriptive analytics. The tools and topics covered under each area of these analytics along with their applications in decision-making process are discussed in this volume. This volume focuses on the descriptive analytics.

This text outlines the broad view of BI that constitutes not only BA but also data analytics, and advanced analytics. An overview of all these areas is presented in the first two chapters followed by the details of BA, which is the focus of this text. The topics and the chapters contained in the first volume are described in the following. The text provides an overview of BA, data analytics, BI, and the descriptive analytics topics. The specific chapters are listed as follows:

(1) Business Analytics (BA) at a Glance
(2) Business Intelligence (BI), Data Analytics, and Business Analytics (BA)
(3) Data, Data Types, and Descriptive Statistics
(4) Data Visualization and Data Visualization Tools

(5) Data Visualization with Big Data
(6) Basic Descriptive Analytics Tools—Describing Data
    Numerically: Concepts and Computer Applications
(7) Wrap-up, Cases, and Notes on Implementation

The Intended Audience

The book is appropriate for majors in business, statistics, graduate students in business, MBAs, professional MBAs and working people in business and industry who are interested in learning and applying the tools of BA in making effective business decisions. The tools of BA are proven to be effective in making timely business decisions and predicting the future outcomes in the current competitive business environment.

The book is designed with a wide variety of audience in mind. It takes a unique approach of presenting the body of knowledge and integrating such knowledge to different areas of BA and predictive modeling. The importance of computer in presenting, analyzing, solving different models is emphasized throughout the book. It takes a simple yet unique learner-centered approach in teaching the BA and predictive modeling tools. The students in information systems interested in analytics and its applications will also find the book to be useful.

Acknowledgments

I would like to thank the reviewers who took the time to provide excellent insights, which helped, shape this book.

I would especially like to thank Mr. Karun Mehta, a friend and engineer. I greatly appreciate the numerous hours he spent in correcting, formatting, and supplying distinctive comments. The book would not be possible without his tireless effort. Karun has been a wonderful friend, counsel, and advisor.

I would like to express my gratitude to Prof. Susumu Kasai, professor of CSIS for reviewing, and administering invaluable suggestions.
I am very thankful to Prof. Edward Engh for his thoughtful advice and counsel.

Special thanks go to Mr. Anand Kumar, Domain Transformation Leader at the Tata Consulting Services (TCS) for reviewing and providing invaluable suggestions. His field and consulting experience in analytical methods greatly helped shape this book.

Thanks to all of my students for their input in making this book possible. They have helped me pursue a dream filled with lifelong learning. This book won't be a reality without them.

I am indebted to senior acquisitions editor, Scott Isenberg; Sheri Dean, director of marketing, all the reviewers, and the publishing team at Business Expert Press for their counsel and support during the preparation of this book. I also wish to thank Mark Ferguson, Editor for reviewing the manuscript and providing helpful suggestions for improvement. I acknowledge the help and support of Exeter Premedia Services, Chennai, India team for their help with editing and publishing.

I would like to thank my parents who always emphasized the importance of what education brings to the world. Lastly, I would like to express a special appreciation to my lovely wife Nilima, to my daughter Neha and her husband Dave, my daughter Smita, and my son Rajeev—both engineers for their creative comments and suggestions. I am grateful for their love, support, and encouragement.

PART I

Foundations of Business Analytics (BA)

CHAPTER 1

Business Analytics (BA) at a Glance

Chapter Highlights

Introduction to Business Analytics

Business Analytics and Its Importance in Modern Business Decisions

Types of Business Analytics

Tools of Business Analytics

Descriptive Analytics: Graphical and Numerical Methods in BA

Tools of Descriptive Analytics

Predictive Analytics

Most Widely Used Predictive Analytics Models

Data Mining, Regression Models, and Time Series Forecasting

Other Predictive Analytics Models

Recent Applications and Tools of Predictive Modeling

Clustering, Classification

Other Areas Associated with Predictive Modeling

Data Mining, Machine Learning, Neural Network, and Deep Learning

Prescriptive Analytics and Tools of Prescriptive Analytics

Applications and Implementation

Summary and Application of Business Analytics (BA) Tools:
Analytical Models and Decision Making Using Models

Glossary of Terms Related to Analytics

Summary

Introduction to Business Analytics

A recent trend in data analysis is the emerging field of *business analytics (BA)*.

This book deals with BA—an emerging area in modern business decision making.

BA is a data driven decision making approach that uses statistical and quantitative analysis, information technology, and management science (mathematical modeling, simulation), along with data mining and fact-based data to measure past business performance to guide an organization in business planning and effective decision making.

BA tools are also used to visualize and explore the patterns and trends in the data to predict future business outcomes with the help of forecasting and predictive modeling.

In this age of technology, companies collect massive amount of data. Successful companies use their data as an asset and use them for competitive advantage. Most businesses collect and analyze massive amounts of data referred to as *Big Data* using specially designed big data software and *data analytics*. Big data analysis is now becoming an integral part of BA.

The companies use BA tools as an organizational commitment to data-driven decision making. BA helps businesses in making informed business decisions. It is also critical in automating and optimizing business processes.

BA makes extensive use of data and descriptive statistics, statistical analysis, mathematical and statistical modeling, and data mining to explore, investigate and understand the business performance. Through data, BA helps to gain insight and drive business planning and decisions. The tools of BA focus on understanding business performance based on the data and a number of models derived from statistics, management science, and operations research areas.

BA also uses statistical, mathematical, optimization, and quantitative tools for explanatory and predictive modeling [1].

Predictive modeling uses statistical models, such as, different types of regression to predict outcomes [2] and is synonymous with the field of data mining and machine learning. It is also referred to as *predictive analytics*. We will provide more details and tools of predictive analytics in subsequent sections.

Business Analytics and Its Importance in Modern Business Decision

BA helps to address, explore and answer a number of questions that are critical in driving business decisions. It tries to answer the following questions:

What is happening and Why did something happen?
Will it happen again?
What will happen if we make changes to some of the inputs?
What the data is telling us that we were not able to see before?

BA uses statistical analysis and predictive modeling to establish trends, figuring out *why* things are happening, and making a prediction about how things will turn out in the future.

BA combines advanced statistical analysis and predictive modeling to give us an idea of what to expect so that you can anticipate developments or make changes now to improve outcomes.

BA is more about anticipated future trends of the key performance indicators. This is about using the past data and models to make predictions. This is different from the reporting in business intelligence (BI). Analytics models use the data with a view to drawing out new, useful insights to improve business planning and boost future performance. BA helps the company adapt to the changes and take advantage of future developments.

One of the major tools of analytics is *Data Mining*, which is a part of predictive analytics. In business, data mining is used to analyze business data. Business transaction data along with other customer and product related data are continuously stored in the databases. The data mining software are used to analyze the vast amount of customer data to reveal hidden patterns, trends, and other customer behavior. Businesses use data mining to perform market analysis to identify and develop new products, analyze their supply chain, find the root cause of manufacturing problems, study the customer behavior for product promotion, improve sales by understanding the needs and requirements of their customer, prevent customer attrition and acquire new customers. For example, Wal-Mart collects and processes over 20 million point-of-sale transactions every day. These data are stored in a centralized database, and are analyzed using data mining software to understand and determine customer behavior, needs and requirements. The data are analyzed to determine sales trends and forecasts, develop marketing strategies, and predict customer-buying habits [http://laits.utexas.edu/~anorman/BUS. FOR/course.mat/Alex/].

A large amount of data and information about products, companies, and individuals are available through **Google, Facebook, Amazon**, and several other sources. Data mining and analytics tools are used to extract meaningful information and pattern to learn customer behavior. Financial institutions analyze data of millions of customers to assess risk and customer behavior. Data mining techniques are also used widely in the areas of science and engineering, such as bioinformatics, genetics, medicine, education, and electrical power engineering.

BA, data analytics, and advanced analytics are growing areas. They all come under the broad umbrella of *BI*. There is going to be an increasing demand of professionals trained in these areas. Many of the tools of data analysis and statistics discussed here are prerequisite to understanding data mining and BA. We will describe the analytics tools including data analytics, advanced analytics later in this chapter.

Types of Business Analytics

The BA area can be divided into different categories depending upon the types of analytics and tools being used. The major categories of BA are:

- Descriptive analytics
- Predictive analytics
- Prescriptive analytics

Each of the previous categories uses different tools and the use of these analytics depends on the type of business and the operations a company is involved in. For example, an organization may only use descriptive analytics tools; whereas another company may use a combination of descriptive and predictive modeling and analytics to predict future business performance to drive business decisions. Other companies may use prescriptive analytics to optimize business processes.

Tools of Business Analytics

The different types of analytics and the tools used in each.

1. **Descriptive analytics: graphical and numerical methods and tools in BA**

   Descriptive analytics involves the use of descriptive statistics including the graphical and numerical methods to describe the data.

   Descriptive analytics tools are used to understand the occurrence of certain business phenomenon or outcomes and explain these outcomes through graphical, quantitative and numerical analysis. Through the visual and simple analysis using the collected data we can visualize and explore what has been happening and the possible reasons for the occurrence of certain phenomenon. Many of the hidden patterns and features not apparent through mere examination of data can be exposed through graphical and numerical analysis. Descriptive analytics uses simple tools to uncover many of the problems quickly and easily. The results enable us question many of the outcomes so that corrective actions can be taken.

   Successful use and implementation of descriptive analytics requires the understanding of types of data, graphical/visual representation of data, and graphical techniques using computer. The graphical and visual techniques are explained in detail in Chapter 4. The descriptive analytics tools include the commonly used graphs and charts along with some newly developed graphical tools such as, bullet graphs, tree maps, and data dashboards. Dashboards are now becoming very popular with big data. They are used to display the multiple views of the business data graphically.

   The other aspect of descriptive analytics is an understanding of numerical methods including the measures of central tendency, measures of position, measures of variation, and measures of shape, and how different measures and statistics are used to draw conclusions and make decision from the data. Some other topics of interest are the understanding of Empirical Rule and the relationship between two variables—the covariance, and correlation coefficient. The tools of descriptive analytics are helpful in understanding the data, identifying

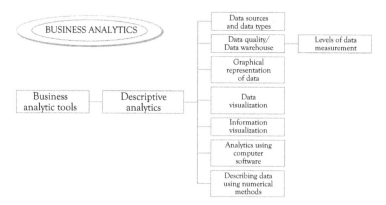

Figure 1.1 Tools of descriptive analytics

the trend or patterns in the data, and making sense from the data contained in the databases of companies. The understanding of databases, data warehouse, web search and query, and big data concepts are important in extracting and applying descriptive analytics tools.

Tools of Descriptive Analytics: Figure 1.1 outlines the tools and methods used in descriptive analytics. These tools are explained in subsequent chapters.

2. Predictive analytics

Predictive Analytics: As the name suggests predictive analytics is the application of predictive models to predict future business outcomes and trends.

Most Widely Used Predictive Analytics Models

The most widely used predictive analytics models are regression, forecasting, and data mining techniques. These are briefly explained in the following.

Data mining techniques are used to extract useful information from huge amounts of data using predictive analytics, computer algorithms, software, mathematical, and statistical tools.

Regression models are used for predicting the future outcomes. Variations of regression models include: (a) Simple regression models, (b) Multiple regression models, (c) Non-linear regression models including the quadratic or second-order models, and polynomial regression models, (d) Regression models with indicator or qualitative independent variables, and (e) Regression models with interaction terms or interaction models.

Regression models are one of the most widely used models in various types of applications. These models are used to explain the relationship between a response variable and one or more independent variables. The relationship may be linear or curvilinear. The objective of these regression models is to predict the response variable using one or more independent variables or predictors.

Forecasting techniques are widely used predictive models that involve a class of *Time Series Analysis and Forecasting models*. The commonly used forecasting models are regression based models that uses regression analysis to forecast future trend. Other time series forecasting models are simple moving average, moving average with trend, exponential smoothing, exponential smoothing with trend, and forecasting seasonal data. All these predictive models are used to forecast the future trend. Figure 1.2 shows the widely used tools of predictive analytics.

Other Predictive Analytics Tools

Besides the tools described in Figure 1.2, an understanding of a number of other analytics tools is critical in describing and drawing meaningful conclusions from the data. These include: (a) Probability

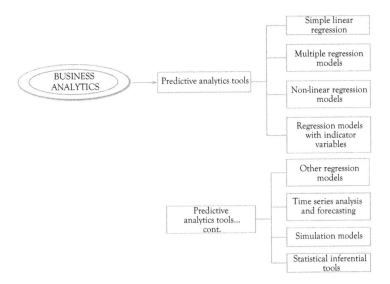

Figure 1.2 Tools of predictive analytics

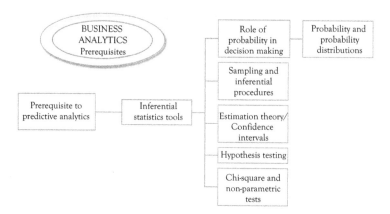

Figure 1.3 Prerequisite to predictive analytics

theory and its role in decision making, (b) Sampling and inference procedures, (c) Estimation and confidence intervals, (d) Hypothesis testing/inference procedures for one and two population parameters, and (e) Chi-square and non-parametric tests. The understanding of these tools is critical in understanding and applying inferential statistics tools—a critical part of data analysis and decision making. These tools are outlined in Figure 1.3.

Additional Tools and Applications of Predictive Analytics

Predictive analytics methods are also used in detecting *anomalies (or outlier) detection, patterns, association learning,* and the concepts of classification and clustering to predict the probabilities and future business outcomes. We briefly describe here anomaly, association learning, classification, and clustering. Figure 1.4 shows the broad categories and applications of predictive analytics.

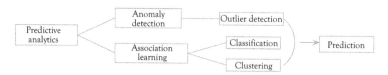

Figure 1.4 Categories of predictive analytics

Association learning is used to identify the items that may co-occur and the possible reasons for their co-occurrence. Classification and clustering techniques are used for association learning.

Anomaly detection is also known as outlier detection and is used to identify specific events, or items, which do not conform to usual or expected pattern in the data. Typical example would be the detection of bank fraud.

Classification and clustering algorithms are used to divide the data into categories or classes. The purpose is to predict the probabilities of future outcomes based on the classification. Clustering and classification both divide the data into classes and therefore, seem to be similar but they are two different techniques. They are learning techniques used widely to obtain reliable information from a collection of raw data. Classification and clustering are widely used in data mining.

Classification

Classification is a process of assigning items to pre specified classes or categories. For example, a financial institution may study the potential borrowers to predict whether a group of new borrowers may be classified as having a high degree of risk. Spam filtering is another example of classification, where the inputs are e-mail messages that are classified into classes as "spam" and "no spam."

Classification uses the algorithms to categorize the new data according to the observations of the training set. *Classification is a supervised learning technique* where a training set is used to find similarities in classes. This means that the input data are divided into two or more classes or categories and the learner creates a model that assigns inputs to one or more of these classes. This is typically done in a supervised way. The objects are classified on the basis of the training set of data.

The algorithm that implements classification is known as the classifier. Some of the most commonly used classification algorithms are K-Nearest Neighbor algorithm and decision tree algorithms. These are widely used in data mining. An example of classification would be credit card processing. A credit card company may want to segment customer database based on similar buying patterns.

Clustering

Clustering technique is used to find natural groupings or clusters in a set of data without pre specifying a set of categories. It is unlike classification where the objects are classified based on pre specified classes or categories. Thus, clustering is an *unsupervised learning technique* where a training set is not used. It uses statistical tools and concepts to create clusters with similar features within the data. Some examples of clustering are:

- Cluster of houses in a town into neighborhoods based on similar features like houses with overall value of over million dollars.
- Marketing analyst may define distinct groups in their customer bases to develop targeted marketing programs.
- City-planning may be interested in identifying groups of houses according to their house value, type, and location.
- In cellular manufacturing, the clustering algorithms are used to form the clusters of similar machines and processes to form machine-component cells.
- Scientists and Geologists may study the Earthquake epicenters to identify clusters of fault lines with high probability of possible earthquake occurrences.

Main Article: Cluster Analysis

Cluster analysis is the assignment of a set of observations into subsets (called *clusters*) so that observations within the same cluster are similar according to some pre specified criterion or criteria, while observations drawn from different clusters are dissimilar. Clustering techniques differ in application and make different assumptions on the structure of the data. In clustering, the clusters are commonly defined by some *similarity metric or similarity coefficient* and may be evaluated by *internal compactness* (similarity between members of the same cluster) and *separation* between different clusters. Other clustering methods are based on *estimated density* and *graph connectivity*. It is important to note that clustering is *unsupervised learning*, and commonly used method in *statistical data analysis*.

The Difference Between Clustering and Classification

Clustering is an unsupervised learning technique used to find groups or clusters of similar instances on the basis of features. The purpose of clustering is a process of grouping similar objects to determine whether there is any relationship between them. *Classification* is a supervised learning technique used to find similarities in classification based on a training set. It uses algorithms to categorize the new data according to the observations in the training set.

Other Areas Associated with Predictive Analytics

Figure 1.5 outlines recent applications and tools of predictive analytics.

The tools outlined in the Figure 1.5 are briefly explained in the following. Extensive applications have emerged in recent years using these methods, which are hot topics of research. A number of applications in business, engineering, manufacturing, medicine, signal processing, and computer engineering using machine learning, neural networks, and deep learning are being reported.

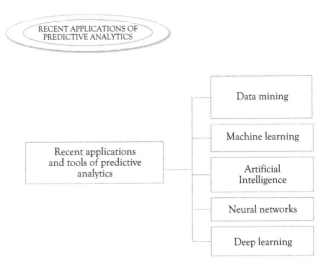

Figure 1.5 Recent applications and tools of predictive modeling

Machine Learning, Data Mining, and Neural Networks

https://en.wikipedia.org/wiki/Machine_learning

In the broad area of data and predictive analytics, machine learning is a method used to develop complex models and algorithms that are used to make predictions. The analytical models in machine learning allow the analysts to make predictions by learning from the trends, patterns, and relationships in the historical data. Machine learning automates model building. The algorithms in machine learning are designed to learn iteratively from data without being programmed.

According to *Arthur Samuel*, machine learning gives "computers the ability to learn without being explicitly programmed."[3][4] Samuel, an American pioneer in the field of *computer gaming* and artificial intelligence, coined the term "machine learning" in 1959 while at IBM.

Machine learning algorithms are extensively used for data-driven predictions and in decision making. Some applications where machine learning has been used are e-mail filtering, detection of network intruders or detecting a data breach, optical character recognition (OCR), learning to rank, and computer vision. Machine learning is employed in a range of computing tasks. Often designing and programming explicit algorithms that are reproducible and have repeatability with good performance is difficult or infeasible.

Machine Learning and Data Mining

Machine learning and data mining are similar in some ways and often overlap in applications. Machine learning is used for prediction, based on *known* properties learned from the training data; whereas data mining algorithms are used for discovery of (previously) *unknown* patterns. Data mining is concerned with knowledge discovery in databases (KDD).

Data mining uses many machine learning methods. On the other hand, machine learning also employs data mining methods as "unsupervised learning" or as a preprocessing step to improve learner accuracy. The goals are somewhat different. The performance of the machine learning is usually evaluated with respect to the ability to *reproduce known* knowledge. In data mining, which is knowledge discovery from the data (KDD) the key task is the discovery of previously *unknown* knowledge. Unlike machine learning which is evaluated with respect to known knowledge, data mining uses uninformed or unsupervised methods that often outperform compared to other supervised methods. In a typical KDD task, supervised methods cannot be used due to the unavailability of training data.

Machine Learning Tasks

Machine learning tasks are typically classified into following three broad categories, depending on the nature of the learning "signal" or "feedback" available to a learning system. These are [5]:

- **Supervised learning**: The computer is presented with example inputs and their desired outputs, given by the analyst, and the goal is to learn a general rule that maps inputs to outputs.
- **Unsupervised learning**: As the name suggests, in unsupervised learning, no labels are given to the program. The learning algorithm is expected to find the structure in its input. The goals of unsupervised learning may be finding hidden pattern in the large data. Thus, unsupervised learning process is not based on general rule of training the algorithms.
- **Reinforcement learning**: In this type of learning, the designed computer program interacts with a dynamic environment in which it has a specific goal to perform. This differs from standard supervised learning as no input/output pairs are provided which involves finding a balance between exploration (of uncharted territory) and exploitation (of current knowledge) [6]. Examples of reinforced learning are playing a game against an opponent. In this type of learning, the computer program is provided feedback in terms of rewards and punishments as it navigates its problem space.

Another application of machine learning is in the area of *deep learning* which is based on artificial *neural networks* (ANNs). In these applications, the learning tasks may contain more than one hidden layer or tasks that contain a single hidden layer known as shallow learning.

Another categorization of machine learning tasks arises when one considers the desired *output* of a machine-learned system:[7] Some of these are classification, clustering, and regression.

- In *classification*, inputs are divided into two or more classes, and the learner must produce a model that assigns unseen inputs to one or more (multi-label classification) of these classes. This is typically tackled in a supervised way. Spam filtering is an example of classification, where the inputs are e-mail (or other) messages and the classes are "spam" and "not spam."
- In *regression*, also a supervised problem, the outputs are continuous rather than discrete. Various types of regression models are used based on the objectives.
- In *clustering*, a set of inputs is to be divided into groups. Unlike in classification, the groups are not known beforehand, making this typically an unsupervised task.
- Machine learning and *statistics* are closely related fields.

Artificial Neural Networks

Main Article: Artificial Neural Network

An ANN learning algorithm, usually called "neural network" (NN), is a learning algorithm that is inspired by the structure and functional aspects of biological neural networks. Computations are structured in terms of an interconnected group of *artificial neurons*, processing information using a connectionist approach to computation. Modern neural networks are non-linear statistical data modeling tools. They are usually used to model complex relationships between inputs and outputs, to find patterns in data, or to capture the statistical structure in an unknown joint probability distribution between observed variables.

Deep Learning

Main Article: *Deep Learning*

Falling hardware prices and the development of Graphics Processing Unit (GPU) for personal use in the last few years have contributed to the development of the concept of *deep learning* which consists of multiple hidden layers in an ANN. This approach tries to model the way the human brain processes light and sound into vision and hearing. Some successful applications of deep learning are *computer vision* and *speech recognition* [8].

> *Note: Neural networks use machine learning algorithms extensively; whereas machine leaning is an application* of artificial intelligence *that automates analytical model building by using algorithms that iteratively learn from data without being explicitly programmed* [9].

Prescriptive Analytics tools are used to optimize certain business process and use a number of different tools that depend on specific application area. Some of these tools are explained here.

Prescriptive analytics is concerned with optimal allocation of resources in an organization. A number of operations research and management science tools have been applied for allocating the limited resources in the most effective way. The operations management tools that are derived from management science and industrial engineering including the simulation tools have also been used to study different types of manufacturing and service organizations. These are proven tools and techniques in studying and understanding the operations and processes of organizations. The tools of operations management can be divided into mainly three areas. These are (a) planning, (b) analysis, and (c) control tools. The analysis part is the prescriptive analysis part that uses the operations research, management science, and simulation tools. The control part is used to monitor and control the product and service quality. There are a number of prescriptive analytics tool in use today. The prescriptive analytics models are shown in Figure 1.6.

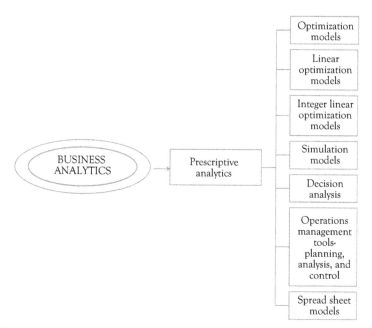

Figure 1.6 Prescriptive analytics tools

Figure 1.7 outlines the tools of descriptive, predictive, and prescriptive analytics tools together. This flow chart is helpful in outlining the difference and details of the tools for each type of analytics. The flow chart in Figure 1.7 shows the vast areas of BA that come under the umbrella of BI.

Applications and Implementation

BA practice deals with extraction, exploration, and analysis of a company's information in order to make effective and timely decisions. The information to make decisions is contained in the data. The companies collect enormous amounts of data that must be processed and analyzed using appropriate means to draw meaningful conclusions.

Much of the analysis using data and information can be attributed to statistical analysis. In addition to the statistical tools, BA uses predictive modeling tools. Predictive modeling uses data mining techniques including anomaly or outlier detection, techniques of classification, and clustering, and different types of regression and forecasting models to predict future business outcomes. Another set of powerful tools in analytics is

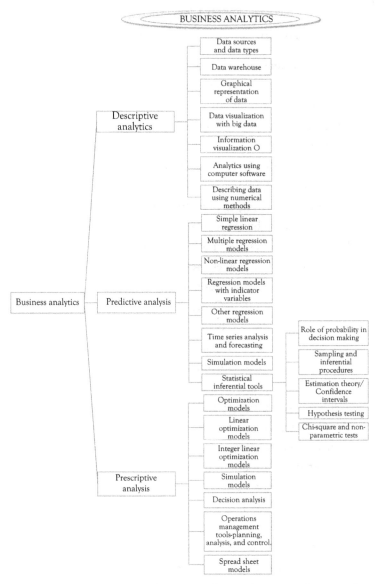

Figure 1.7 Descriptive, predictive, and prescriptive analytics tools

prescriptive modeling tools. These include optimization and simulation tools to optimize business processes.

While the major objective of BA is to empower companies to make data-driven decisions; it also helps companies to automate and optimize business processes and operations.

Summary and Application of Business Analytics (BA) Tools

- **Descriptive analytics** tools uses statistical, graphical, and numerical methods to understand the occurrence of certain business phenomenon. These simple tools of descriptive analytics are very helpful in explaining the vast amount of data collected by businesses. The quantitative, graphical, and visual tools along with simple numerical methods provide insights that are very helpful in data driven fact-based decisions.

- **Predictive modeling or predictive analytics** tools are used to predict future business phenomenon. Predictive models have many applications in business. Some examples include the spam detection in messages and fraud detection. It has been used in outlier detection in the data that can point toward fraud detection. Other areas were predictive modeling tools have been used or being used are customer relationship management (CRM) and predicting customer behavior and buying patterns, Other applications are in the areas of engineering, management, capacity planning, change management, disaster recovery, digital security management, and city planning. One of the major applications of predictive modeling is data mining. *Data mining* involves exploring new patterns and relationships from the collected data.

  Data mining is a part of predictive analytics. It involves analyzing massive amount of data. In this age of technology, businesses collect and store massive amount of data at enormous speed every day. It has become increasingly important to process and analyze the huge amount of data to extract useful information and patterns hidden in the data. The overall goal of data mining is knowledge discovery from the data. Data mining involves (i) extracting previously unknown and potential useful knowledge or patterns from massive amount of data collected and stored, and (ii) exploring and analyzing these large quantities of data to discover meaningful pattern and transforming data into an understandable structure for further use. The field of data mining is rapidly growing and statistics plays a major role in it. Data mining is also known as KDD, pattern analysis, information harvesting, BI, BA, and so on. Besides statistics, data mining uses artificial intelligence, machine learning, data base systems and advanced statistical tools, and pattern recognition.

• **Prescriptive analytics** tools have applications in optimizing and automating business processes. Prescriptive analytics is concerned with optimal allocation of resources in an organization. A number of operations research and management science tools are used for allocating limited resources in the most effective way. The common prescriptive analytics tools are linear and non-linear optimization model including linear programming, integer programming, transportation, assignment, scheduling problems, 0-1 programming, simulation problems, and many others. Many of the operations management tools that are derived from management science and industrial engineering including the simulation tools are also part of prescriptive analytics.

Analytical Models and Decision Making Using Models

A major part of analytics is about solving problems using different types of models. The following are the most commonly used models and are parts of descriptive, predictive, or prescriptive analytics models. Some of these models are listed as follows and will be discussed later.

Types of Models

1. Graphical models
2. Quantitative models
3. Algebraic models
4. Spreadsheet models
5. Simulation models
6. Process modeling
7. Other analytic models—predictive and prescriptive model

Overview of This Volume

This first volume of the book deals with an overview of the field of BI and BA. The first two chapters of the book provided a detailed discussion and an introduction to BA, importance of analytics in business decisions, types of BA—descriptive, predictive, and prescriptive and an overview of the tools used in each one. This volume introduces the field of analytics including BA, BI, data analytics, and provides a complete treatment of descriptive analytics applications. It also outlines a list of the tools used in predictive and prescriptive analytics and their functions.

This first volume of the book discusses the details of descriptive analytics and outlines the tools of predictive and prescriptive analytics. The predictive analytics is about predicting the future business outcomes, while the prescriptive analytics is about optimizing certain business activities. A complete treatment of the topics used in predictive and prescriptive analytics is not possible in one brief volume of analytics book, therefore, these are covered in volume II of this book.

Preview of Volume II of This Book

The second volume of this book is a continuation of this first volume and is entitled:

Business Analytics: A Data Driven Decision Making Approach for Business: Volume II

The focus of the second volume is predictive analytics, its purpose, applications, and the tools used in this analytics. This volume will cover the following predictive analytics topics:

Content of Volume II:

1. *Introduction to Predictive Analytics*
2. *Background and Prerequisites for Predictive Modeling*
   (a) Probability distributions and its role in decision making, (b) Sampling and inference procedures, (c) Estimation and confidence intervals, (d) Hypothesis testing/inference procedures for one and

two population parameters, and (e) Introduction to Chi-square and non-parametric tests

3. *Most Widely used Predictive Analytics Models*

The most widely used predictive analytics models are regression, forecasting, data mining techniques, and simulation. These topics are discussed in detail.

4. *Regression and Correlation Analysis*

- Regression models as one of the most widely used models in various types of applications.
- Models used to explain the relationship between a response variable and one or more independent variables.

5. *Linear and Non-linear Regression*

6. *Regression Models*:

1. Introduction to regression
2. Variations of regression models include:
   - Simple regression models;
   - Multiple regression models;
   - Non-linear regression models including the quadratic or second-order models, and polynomial regression models;
   - Regression models with indicator or qualitative independent variables; and
   - Regression models with interaction terms or interaction models.

7. *Forecasting Techniques:*

- *Time series analysis and forecasting models*
- Commonly used forecasting models
- Regression based models or associative models
- Time series forecasting models based on averages
- Simple moving average, moving average with trend, exponential smoothing, exponential smoothing with trend, and forecasting seasonal data

8. *Data Mining*

- Introduction to Data Mining
- Techniques are used to extract useful information from huge amounts of data using predictive analytics, computer algorithms, software, mathematical, and statistical tools

- Types of information: association, classification, clustering, forecasting, and sequence
- Data Mining applications and case

9. ***Simulations and Their Applications***

   Case Analysis on Predictive Analytics

   Analytical Models

   Most commonly used models of descriptive, predictive, or prescriptive analytics

   1. Graphical models
   2. Quantitative models
   3. Algebraic models
   4. Spreadsheet models
   5. Simulation models
   6. Process modeling

   Introduction to Other Areas Associated with Predictive Analytics

   - Recent applications and research areas:
     - Data mining, machine learning, neural network, and deep learning.
   - Recent examples and applications of predictive modeling
     - Some examples of the applications of predictive modeling in business, engineering, manufacturing, medicine, signal processing and computer engineering using machine learning, neural networks, and deep learning.

10. ***Introduction to Prescriptive Analytics and Tools***

Summary

BA uses data, statistical analysis, mathematical and statistical modeling, data mining, and advanced analytics tools including forecasting and simulation to explore, investigate and understand the business performance. Through data, BA helps to gain insight and drive business planning and decisions. The tools of BA focus on understanding business performance based on the data and a number of models derived from statistics, management science, and different types of analytics tools.

BA helps companies to make informed business decisions and can be used to automate and optimize business processes. Data-driven companies treat their data as a corporate asset and leverage it for competitive advantage. Successful BA depends on *data quality* and skilled analysts who understand the technologies. BA is an organizational commitment to data-driven decision making.

This chapter provided an overview of the field of BA. The tools of BA including the descriptive, predictive, and prescriptive analytics along with advanced analytics tools were discussed. The chapter also introduced a number of terms related to and used in conjunction with BA. Flow diagrams outlining the tools of each of the descriptive, predictive, and prescriptive analytics were presented. Finally, this chapter provided an overview of this first volume of the book. The volume II of this book is a continuation of this first volume. A preview of the second volume entitled: *Business Analytics: A Data Driven Decision Making Approach for Business: Volume II was outlined in this chapter.*

Glossary of Terms Related to Analytics

Big Data

Big data is a collection of data sets so large and complex that it becomes difficult to process using on-hand database management tools or traditional data processing application [Wikipedia]. Most businesses collect and analyze massive amounts of data referred to as *Big Data* using specially designed big data software and *data analytics*. Big data analysis is integral part of BA.

Big Data Definition (As per O'Reilly Media)

Big data is data that exceeds the processing capacity of conventional database systems. The data is too big, moves too fast, or doesn't fit the structures of your database architectures. To gain value from this data, you must choose an alternative way to process it.

Gartner was credited with the 3 'V's of Big Data. Gartner's Big Data is: High-volume, high-velocity and/or high-variety information assets that demand cost-effective, innovative forms of information processing that enable enhanced insight, decision making, and process automation.

Gartner is referring to the size of data (large volume), speed with which the data is being generated (velocity), and the different types of data (variety) and this seemed to align with the combined definition of Wikipedia and O'Reilly media.

Mike Gualtieri of Forrester said that the 3 'V's mentioned by Gartner are just measures of data. He insisted that following definition is more actionable and can be seen as:

Big data is the frontier of a firm's ability to store, process, and access (SPA) all the data it needs to operate effectively, make decisions, reduce risks, and serve customers.

Algorithm: A mathematical formula or statistical process used to analyze data.

Analytics: Involves drawing insights from the data including big data. Analytics uses simple to advanced tools depending upon the objectives. Analytics may involve visual display of data (charts and graphs), descriptive statistics, making predictions, forecasting future outcomes, or optimizing business processes. The more recent terms is *Big Data Analytics* that involves making inferences using very large sets of data. Thus, analytics can take different form depending on the objectives and the decisions to be made. They may be descriptive, predictive, or prescriptive analytics. These are briefly described here.

Descriptive Analytics: If you are using charts and graphs or time series plots to study the demand or the sales patterns, or the trend for the stock market you are using descriptive analytics. Also, calculating statistics from the data such as, the mean, variance, median, or percentiles are all examples of descriptive analytics. Some of the recent software are designed to create dashboards that are useful in analyzing business outcomes. The dashboards are examples of descriptive analytics. Of course, a lot of more details can be created from the data by plotting and performing simple analyzes.

Predictive Analytics: As the name suggests, predictive analytics is about predicting the future outcomes. It also involves forecasting demand, sales, and profits for a company. The commonly used techniques for predictive analytics are different types of regression and forecasting models. Some advanced techniques are data mining, machine learning, neural networks, and advanced statistical models. We will discuss the regression and forecasting techniques as well as the terms later in this book.

Prescriptive Analytics: Prescriptive analytics involves analyzing the results of the predictive analytics and "prescribes" the best category to target and minimize or maximize the objective (s). It builds on predictive analytics and often suggests the best course of action leading to best possible solution. It is about optimizing (maximizing or minimizing) an objective function. The tools of prescriptive analytics are now used with big data to make data-driven decisions by selecting the best course of actions involving multi-criteria decision variables. Some examples of prescriptive analytics models are linear and nonlinear optimization models, different types of simulations, and others.

Data Mining: Data mining involves finding meaningful patterns and deriving insights from large data sets. It is closely related to analytics. Data mining uses statistics, machine learning, and artificial intelligence techniques to derive meaningful patterns.

Analytical Models: Most commonly used models that are parts of descriptive, predictive, or prescriptive analytics are;

Graphical models, quantitative models, algebraic models, spreadsheet models, simulation models, process models, other analytic models—predictive and prescriptive models.

IOT stands for Internet of Things (IOT). It means the interconnection of computing devices in embedded objects (sensors, cars, fridges, etc.) via Internet with capabilities of sending/receiving data. The devices in IOT generate huge amounts of data providing opportunities for big data applications and data analytics opportunities.

Machine Learning: Machine learning is a method of designing systems that can learn, adjust, and improve based on the data fed to them. Machine learning works based on predictive and statistical algorithms that are provided to these machines. The algorithms are designed to learn and improve as more data flows through the system. Fraud detection, e-mail spam, and GPS systems are some examples of machine learning applications.

R: "R" is a programming language for statistical computing. It is one of the popular languages in data science.

Structured versus Unstructured Data: refer to the "Volume" and "Variety"—the 'V's of Big Data structured data is the data that can be stored in the relational databases. This type of data can be analyzed and organized in such a way that can be related to other data via tables. Unstructured data cannot be directly put in the data bases or analyzed or organized directly. Some examples are e-mail/text messages, social media posts and recorded human speech, and so on.

CHAPTER 2

Business Intelligence (BI), Business Analytics (BA), and Data Analytics

Chapter Highlights

Introduction: Analytics, Business Analytics, and Business Intelligence

Business Intelligence (BI)

Business Intelligence (BI): Defined

Additional Tools of BI

Advanced Analytics Tools

BI Functions and Applications Explained

> Reporting   OLAP Business Process Management (BPM)

More Application Areas of Analytics

> Data Mining   Process Mining
> Business Performance Management   Benchmarking
> Text Mining/Text Analytics

Data Analysis and Data Analytics

Requirements of Data Analytics:

Prerequisites to Data Analytics: Data Preparation for Data Analytics

> Data Cleansing, Data Transformation, Scripting, Modeling, and Data
> Warehousing
> Data and Data Quality

Tools and Applications of Data Analytics

Advanced Analytics

BI Programs in Companies

Specific Areas of BI Applications in an Enterprise

Success Factors for BI Applications
Comparing Business Intelligence with Business Analytics
Business Analytics Applied to Different Areas

Web Analytics   Supply Chain Analytics
Marketing Analytics   Human Resource Analytics
Financial Analytics   Applications of Analytics in Other Areas

Difference Between Business Analytics and Business Intelligence
Glossary of Terms Related to Business Intelligence
Summary

Introduction: Analytics, Business Analytics (BA), and Business Intelligence (BI)

In this chapter, we discuss analytics, business intelligence (BI) and business analytics (BA) as decision-making tools in businesses today. Although these terms are used interchangeably but there are slight differences in the terms of the tools they use. The connection between BI and BA tools combined with the applications in the computer science and information technology are critical for the success of BA in a company. This chapter discusses the broad meaning of the terms—BI, BA, data analytics (DA), computer and information technology, and how they are used in business decision making. The chapter also distinguishes between BI and BA, and the specific tools used in each case.

Analytics is the science of analysis—the processes by which we interpret data, draw conclusions, and make decisions. BA goes well beyond simply presenting data and creating visuals, crunching numbers, and computing statistics. The essence of analytics lies in the application—making sense from the data using prescribed methods, tools and logic to draw meaningful conclusion from the data. It uses logic and intelligence, and mental processes that enable us to reason, organize, plan, analyze, solve problems, understand, innovate, learn, and make decisions.

Business analytics (BA) covers a vast area. It is a complex field that encompasses visualization, statistics and statistical modeling, and statistical analysis. It uses descriptive, predictive, and prescriptive analytics including text and speech analytics, web analytics, decision processes and much more.

Business Intelligence (BI) combines a broad set of data analysis applications. It includes applications, such as querying, enterprise reporting, online analytical processing (OLAP), mobile BI, real-time BI, operational BI, and cloud applications. BI technology also includes data visualization software for designing charts and other infographics, as well as tools for building BI dashboards and performance scorecards that display visualized data on business metrics and key performance indicators (KPIs) in an easy-to-grasp way. BI applications can be bought separately from different vendors or as part of a unified BI platform from a single vendor.

BI programs can also incorporate forms of advanced analytics, such as predictive analytics, data mining, text mining, statistical analysis, and big data analytics. In many cases advanced analytics projects are conducted and managed by separate teams of data scientists, statisticians, predictive modelers and other skilled analytics professionals, while BI teams oversee more straightforward querying and analysis of business data.

Business Intelligence (BI)

Business Intelligence (BI) uses a set of techniques, algorithms and tools to analyze raw data from multiple sources in a business. BI tools and methods are helpful in getting insights using data analysis that enables managers to make fact-based decisions.

The overall objectives of the BI and BA programs are similar. Companies are adopting these programs because these are critical in driving business decisions based on the current data. In a broad sense, BI incorporates the tools of BA including the descriptive, predictive, and prescriptive analytics that help companies in data-driven business decisions.

BI comprises of the processes, technologies, strategies, and analytical methods that turn the data or information into knowledge that are critical to driving business decisions. These tools, methods and technologies help companies in running business operations and making fact-based data driven decisions.

In 1989, Howard Dresner (later a Gartner analyst) proposed "business intelligence" as an umbrella term to describe "concepts and methods to improve business decision making by using fact-based support

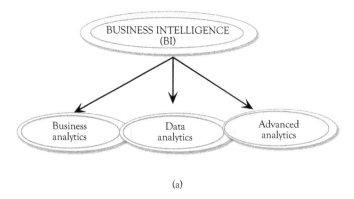

(a)

The broad area of business intelligence (BI)

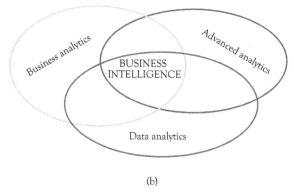

(b)

Figure 2.1 *(a) Business intelligence and support systems.*
(b) Relationship between business intelligence, business analytics,
data analytics, and advanced analytics

systems."[10] It was not until the late 1990s that this usage was widespread
[11]. Figure 2.1(a) shows the broad areas the BI is comprised of.

Figure 2.1(b) shows that BI links BA, DA, and advanced analytics.
The tools in each of these categories overlap and make up the overall
BI process.

Business Intelligence (BI): Defined

According to David Loshin BI is "... *the processes, technologies and tools*
needed to turn data into information, information into knowledge, and
knowledge into plans that drive profitable business actions."

Larissa Moss' "... *an architecture and a collection of integrated operational as well as decision-support applications and databases that provide the business community easy access to business data.*"

BI is a technology-driven process for processing and analyzing data to make sense from huge quantities of data that businesses collect and obtain from various sources. In a broad sense, BI is both visualization and analytics. The purpose of visualization or graphic presentation of data is to obtain meaningful and useful information to help management, business managers and other end users make more informed business decisions. BI uses a wide variety of tools, applications, and methodologies that enable organizations to collect data from internal systems and processes as well as external sources. The collected data may be both structured and unstructured. The first challenge is to prepare the data to run queries, perform analysis, and create reports.

One of the major tasks is to create *dashboards* and other forms of data visualizations and make the analysis results available to corporate decision makers as well as the managers and others involved in the decision making process. [http://searchbusinessanalytics.techtarget.com/definition/business-intelligence-BI]

BI has evolved from mere *business reporting* which involves reporting of operational and financial data by a business enterprise. Reports are generated using powerful and easy-to-use data analysis or DA tools that may be simple to more complex. With the advancement of technology and computing power, visuals and data dashboards are commonly used in business reporting.

The BI tools, technologies and technical architectures are used in the collection, analysis, presentation and dissemination of business information. The analysis of business data provides historical as well as current and future views of the business performance. Specialized data analysis and software are now available that are capable of processing and analyzing big data. They can create multiple views of the business performance in form of dashboards, which are extremely helpful in displaying current business performance. The *big data* software is now being used for analyzing vast amount of data. They are extremely helpful in the decision making process. Besides data visualization, a number of models described earlier are used to predict and optimize future business outcomes.

Applications of Business Intelligence (BI)

BI applications apply software for data visualization, dashboards, info-graphics, and big data analysis software. These tools fall under the descriptive analytics and statistical modeling.

BI also uses a broad range of applications including statistical analysis tools (both descriptive, inferential statistics, and advanced statistical applications).

Data Analysis Applications

Data Analysis Applications and Tools of Business Intelligence (BI)

The data analysis applications include extracting data from the data bases and data warehouse; **querying, reporting, online analytical processing (OLAP), advanced analytics, process mining, business performance management, benchmarking, text mining,** *mobile and real-time BI, cloud based applications, tools for reporting and displaying business metrics, and key performance indicators (KPIs) of business. In addition, the applications of BI include the tools of* predictive and prescriptive analytics. These terms are explained below in the following.

Additional Tools of BI

In addition to the aforementioned applications and reporting, BI uses the tools of *predictive and prescriptive analytics* as well as advanced analytics tools that include data mining applications. Predictive analytics is a broad area of BI. Data mining applications and the growing applications of machine learning and artificial intelligence also come under the broad category of BI although these techniques are more relevant to analytics that comes under the broad umbrella of BI. Big data analytics and a number of optimization and advanced modeling that come under prescriptive analytics are also application areas of BI.

BI technologies are capable of handling large amounts of structured and sometimes unstructured data. The tools of BI are designed for the

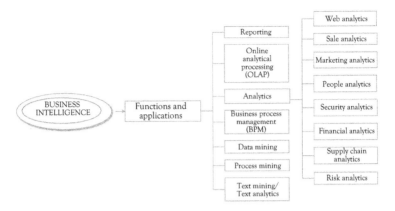

Figure 2.2 Functions and application areas of business intelligence (BI)

analysis and interpretation of massive amounts of data (big data) that help businesses identify potential problems, opportunities for improvement, and develop strategic business plans. These are critical for the businesses to maintain a competitive edge, long-term stability, and improve market share and profitability. BI technologies provide historical, current and predictive views of business operations. Common functions and applications of BI technologies are shown in Figure 2.2. These applications are helpful in developing and creating new strategic business opportunities. The additional *advanced analytics* tools used in BI are shown in Figure 2.3.

Advanced Analytics Tools

BI Functions and Applications Explained

The major areas and functions of BI explained in Figure 2.2 are explained as follows.

Reporting

Business reporting or enterprise reporting is "the reporting of operational and financial data by a business enterprise. It is about providing information to decision-makers within an organization to aid in business decisions."

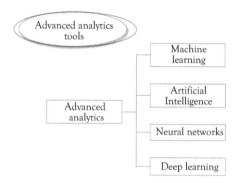

Figure 2.3 Advanced analytics tools

Online Analytical Processing (OLAP)

Online analytical processing, or *OLAP* is a reporting tool and is a part of the broader category of BI. Application of OLAP includes multi-dimensional analytical (MDA) queries in computing and reporting based on relational database, and data mining.

The applications of OLAP also include business reporting for sales, marketing, management reporting, **business process management* (BPM) [12], budgeting forecasting, financial reporting and similar areas. The term *OLAP* was created as a slight modification of the traditional database term online transaction processing (OLTP).

Business Process Management (BPM)

*Business process management (BPM) uses *operations management* tools to manage the internal operations of an organization. It is about the management of production and service systems of a company. It uses various tools and techniques to plan, model, analyze, improve, optimize, control, and automate business processes.

The objective of operations management in a company is to convert inputs (raw materials, labor, and energy) into outputs (in the form of useful products and/or services) using different types of transformation processes.

The tools of operations management are used in allocating the limited resources in the most effective way. They are used in both manufacturing and service organizations to produce products, manage quality and create and manage services. In the services, operation management is used to manage and run the banking systems, and hospitals, to name a few. Operations management has wide application in strategy, management, supply chains, marketing, finance, human resources, and production. Operations management has three broad categories—planning, analysis, and control of business operations and uses a number of tools in each of these phases. It uses forecasting, capacity planning, aggregate planning, materials requirement planning (MRP), product and process designs, strategy, and a number of analysis tools including scheduling, resource allocation, project management, quality and lean six sigma, and others.

The major objective of BPM is on improving business performance by managing processes. A number of software tools and technologies are used in BPM. As an approach, BPM views processes as important assets of an organization that must be capable of delivering value-added products and services to clients or customers. This approach closely resembles Lean Six Sigma, and total quality management methodologies—the objective of which are the removal of waste and defects from any process, service or manufacturing. https://en.wikipedia.org/wiki/Business_process_management

Analytics as discussed in the previous chapter is the use of mathematical and statistical techniques including modeling, computer programming, software applications, and operations research to gain insight from the data.

Organizations may apply analytics to business data to describe, predict, and improve business performance. Specifically, areas within analytics include descriptive analytics, predictive analytics, and prescriptive analytics. Analytics uses extensive descriptive techniques and predictive models to gain valuable knowledge from data.

Analytics is known by different names and it has different forms when applied to different areas. The types of analytics based on applications may be: supply chain analytics, retail analytics, and optimization based (prescriptive analytics), marketing analytics involving marketing optimization and *marketing mix modeling, *web analytics,* sales analytics for sales force sizing and optimization. Analytics require extensive computation using software applications. The algorithms and software used for analytics use methods in computer science, statistics, and mathematics [13].

Web analytics is one of the commonly used analytics related to web data. It frequently appears in the analytics literature and applications. We describe it briefly here.

Web analytics is the collection, analysis and reporting of web data for purposes of understanding and optimizing web usage [14]. However, one of the major applications of web analytics is measuring web traffic. It has a number of applications in almost every field now including marketing, sales, finance, and advertising and is a major tool for business and market research. It is used to estimate how traffic to a website changes when changes in the advertising campaign for a company occur or how the web traffic compares to other businesses in the same class. One of the common and very useful applications of web analytics is keeping track of the number of visitors to a website, the number of pages, and the time spend by the visitors. It also helps monitor and manage traffic flow and popularity, customer behavior and trends which are useful for making future predictions. It is now one of the major tools for market research.

Web analytics is also used to manage, control, analyze, and improve websites using a wide variety of applications and analytical tools. A number of web and business applications using machine learning and artificial intelligence are now being reported. The recent research areas in web analytics include artificial neural networks and deep learning. These tools are applied extensively to study, improve, and predict future business outcomes. Web analytics applications are also used to help companies measure the results of traditional print or broadcast advertising campaigns. It helps one to estimate how traffic to a website changes after the launch of a new product. Web analytics is not limited to the applications mentioned earlier. New applications and tools are emerging as a result of research and development. The newer applications of machine learning, artificial, intelligence, and neural networks are emerging areas of research and are finding new applications.

Steps of Web Analytics: Most web analytics processes can be divided into four essential stages or steps [15], which are:

- Collection of data: This stage is the collection of the basic, elementary data. The objective of this stage is to gather the data which is complex and takes many forms depending on the types of data collected.

- Processing of data into information: Before the data can be of any use, it must be processed.
- Developing KPIs: This stage focuses on using the ratios (and counts) and infusing them with business strategies, referred to as KPIs. Many times, KPIs deal with conversion aspects, but not always. It depends on the organization.
- Formulating online strategy: This stage is concerned with the online goals, objectives, and standards for the organization or business. These strategies are usually related to making money, saving money, or increasing market share.

More Application Areas of Analytics

Data Mining: Data mining and its applications were discussed briefly earlier. It involves exploring new patterns and relationships from the collected data.

Data mining is a part of predictive analytics. It involves processing and analyzing huge amount of data to extract useful information and patterns hidden in the data. The overall goal of data mining is knowledge discovery from the data. Data mining techniques are used to (i) extracting previously unknown and potential useful knowledge or patterns from massive amount of data collected and stored, and (ii) exploring and analyzing these large quantities of data to discover meaningful pattern and transforming data into an understandable structure for further use. The field of data mining is a rapidly growing and statistics plays a major role in it. Data mining is also known as knowledge discovery in databases (KDDs), pattern analysis, information harvesting, BI, BA, and so on. Besides statistics, data mining uses artificial intelligence, machine learning, data base systems and advanced statistical tools, and pattern recognition.

Process Mining: Process mining is a process management technique used to analyze *business processes*. The purpose is to create a better understanding of the processes so that improvement efforts can be directed to improve the process efficiency. Process mining is also known as *automated business process discovery* (ABPD).

Business Performance Management: Business performance management is the management of an organization's performance and comes under the broad category of *business process management (BPM)*. It consists of the activities that ensure that the set goals of the company are consistently met in an effective and efficient manner. The term is synonymously used with corporate performance management (CPM) and enterprise performance management.

The major activities of business performance management are: (1) identification and selection of an organization's goals, (2) a measurement process to measure an organization's progress against the goals, and (3) comparing the actual performance to the set goals and taking corrective actions to improve the future performance.

Business performance management activities involve the collection and reporting of large volumes of data that requires the use of BI software to assist in this process. It is important to note that the business performance management does not necessarily rely on software systems. It is often a misconception that BPM is a software dependent system and BI software is a definitive approach to business performance management.

Benchmarking

Benchmarking is comparing one's business processes, performance metrics, and best practices to the industries with the best in class.

Benchmarking is used to measure performance using a specific indicator. Some examples of these indicators are: cost per unit of measure, productivity per unit of measure, cycle time of x per unit of measure or defects per unit of measure. When measured, these metrics provide a metric of performance that is then compared to others [16].

Benchmarking is also referred to as "best practice benchmarking" or "process benchmarking." The process involves evaluating key performance metrics of an organization's processes in relation to best in class companies' processes. Other application include Text mining.

Text Mining [https://en.wikipedia.org/wiki/Text_mining] is also referred to as *text data mining*. It is somewhat similar to the *text analytics*, which is the process of deriving high-quality information from text. This high quality information is typically derived using patterns and trends using means such as statistical pattern learning.

Text mining usually involves the process of structuring the input text (usually parsing, along with the addition of some derived linguistic features and the removal of others, and subsequent insertion into a database), deriving patterns within the structured data, and finally evaluation and interpretation of the output. "High quality" in text mining usually refers to some combination of relevance (how well a retrieved document or set of documents meets the information need of the user) and interestingness.

Typical text mining tasks include text categorization, text clustering [17], concept/entity extraction, production of granular taxonomies, sentiment analysis, document summarization, and entity relation modeling (i.e., learning relations between named entities).

Text analysis involves information retrieval, lexical analysis to study word frequency distributions, pattern recognition, information extraction, data mining techniques including link and association analysis, visualization, and predictive analytics. The overall goal is to turn text into data for analysis using natural language processing [18] (NLP) and analytical methods.

A typical application is to scan a set of documents written in a *natural language*. It is also known as *ordinary language*—any language that has evolved naturally in humans through use and repetition without conscious planning or premeditation. Natural languages can take different forms, such as speech or signing (sign language). They are distinguished from constructed and formal languages such as those used to program computers or to study logic [19].

Text Analytics

The term *text analytics* describes a set of linguistic applications (the scientific [20] study of languages and involves an analysis of language). It uses statistical and machine learning techniques to model and structure the information content of textual sources. The term is synonymous with text mining. Ronen Feldman modified a 2,000 description of "text mining"[21] in 2004 to describe "text analytics."[22] The latter term is now used more frequently in business settings.

The term text analytics also describes the application of text analytics to respond to business problems, whether independently or in conjunction with query and analysis of fielded, numerical data. In general, approximately 80 percent of business-relevant information originates in unstructured form, primarily text [23]. The techniques of text analytics processes, discover and present knowledge—facts, business rules, and relationships—that is otherwise locked in textual form. [https://en.wikipedia.org/wiki/Text_mining]

Data Analysis and Data Analytics

Data Analysis is the process of systematically applying statistical techniques to collect, describe condense, illustrate, analyze, interpret and evaluate *data*. It is a process of summarizing, organizing, and communicating information using a number of graphical tools including histograms, stem-and-leaf plots, box plots, distribution charts, as well as statistical inferential tools. The methods of displaying data using charts and graphs vary widely including those of displaying big data that often uses dashboards.

Data Analytics is about drawing conclusion by examining and analyzing datasets. It uses specialized systems and software. *Data analytics* techniques are widely used in industries to enable organizations to make more-informed data-driven business decisions.

DA is about extracting meaning from raw data using *specialized computer systems* and software that organize, transform, and model the data to draw conclusions and identify patterns. It is all about running the business in a better way, make data-driven informed decisions (not based on the assumption), improving the market share, and profitability. *Today, DA is often associated with the analysis of large volumes of data and/or high-velocity data, which presents unique data preparation, handling, and computational challenges. DA professionals have expertise in statistics and statistical modeling, and in using data analysis and big data software. The skilled DA professionals are called Data Scientists.*

Data analytics techniques have wide applications in research, medicine, and other areas listed in the following. The techniques are used to draw inference, and to prove or disprove theories and hypotheses. Some of the areas where analytics techniques are being used:

Marketing—gaining customer insights, retail solutions, digital marketing, Internet security, manufacturing and supply chain analytics, science and medicine, engineering, risk management, and financial analysis.

Requirements of Data Analytics

Data analytics involves *cleansing*, organizing, presenting, *transforming*, and *modeling data* to gain insight and discover useful information. One of the most important requirements and criteria of DA is *data quality*.

Prerequisites to Data Analytics: Data Preparation for Data Analytics

Before the data can be used effectively for analysis, the following data preparation steps are essential. These are:

1. Data cleansing;
2. Scripting;
3. Data transformation; and
4. Data warehousing.

Data and Data Quality

In data analysis and analytics, data can be viewed as *information*. Data are also *measurements*. The purpose of data analysis is to make sense from data. Data when collected (in its raw form) is known as *raw data*. These are the data not processed.

In data analysis, data needs to be converted into a form suitable for reporting and analytics. [http://searchdatamanagement.techtarget.com/definition/data]

It is acceptable for data to be used as a singular subject or a plural subject. *Raw data* is a term used to describe data in its most basic digital format.

Data quality is affected by the way data is collected, entered in the system, stored and managed. Efficient and accurate storage (data warehouse), cleansing, and data transformation are critical for assuring data quality. The following are important considerations in assuring data quality Aspects of data quality include: [http://searchdatamanagement. techtarget.com/definition/data-quality]

Accuracy
Completeness
Update status
Relevance
Consistency across data sources
Reliability
Appropriate presentation
Accessibility

Within an organization, acceptable data quality is crucial to operational and transactional processes. These aforementioned are prerequisites to DA and are explained in Chapter 3.

Tools and Applications of Data Analytics

Data analytics predominantly refers to an assortment of applications including:

Basic BI, reporting and OLAP and various forms of advanced analytics. It is similar in nature to BA—which is about analyzing data to make informed data-driven decisions relating to business applications—DA has a broader focus. The expansive view of the term isn't universal, though: *In some cases, people use DA specifically to mean analytics and advanced analytics, treating BI as a separate category. We provide more details of Business Intelligence in the next chapter.*

Advanced Analytics: http://searchbusinessanalytics.techtarget.com/ definition/advanced-analytics

Advanced analytics is a broad category of inquiry that is used for forecasting future trends using simulation that are helpful in conducting *what-if analyses (simulation or risk analysis)* to see the effects of potential changes in business strategies. Simulation and risk analysis are very useful decision making tools under risk and uncertainty. They help drive changes and improvements in business practices.

The analytical categories that fall under advanced analytics are: predictive analytics, data mining, big data analytics, and machine learning applications. These are just some of the analytical categories that fall under the heading of advanced analytics. These technologies are widely used in industries including marketing, healthcare, risk management, and economics.

BI Programs in Companies

BI is most effective when it combines data derived from the market in which a company operates (external data) with data from company sources internal to the business such as financial and operations data (internal data). When combined, external and internal data can provide a more complete picture, which in effect, creates an "intelligence" that cannot be derived by any singular set of data [24].

BI along with BA empower organizations to gain a better understanding of the existing markets and customer behavior. The tools of BI are being used to study the markets, analyze massive amounts of data to learn about customer behavior, conduct risk analysis, assess demand and suitability of products and services for different market segments, predict and optimize business processes to name a few. [https://en.wikipedia.org/wiki/Business_intelligence#cite_note-1]

Specific Areas of BI Applications in an Enterprise

BI can be applied to the following business purposes, in order to drive business decisions and value.

BI applications are applied to:

1. *Performance Measurement* or measurement of performance metrics—program that creates a hierarchy of performance metrics (see also Metrics Reference Model) and benchmarking that informs business leaders about progress toward business goals (business process management).

    Metrics are the variables whose measured values are tied to the performance of the organization. They are also known as the performance metrics because they are performance indicator.

Metrics may be finance based that focus on the performance of the organization. Some metrics are designed to measure requirements and value (customer wants and needs, what the customer wants, satisfaction level, and so on). In manufacturing, metrics are designed to measure the quality level and other key performance. In quality and Six Sigma projects, one of the major metrics is defects per million opportunities (DPMO), percent yield, first pass yield, and sigma level which is an indicator of quality level and parts per million defects. In project management, including Six Sigma projects a number of metrics are measured that help plan, analyze, and control the projects. These metrics may be indicators of time, cost, resources, overall quality and performance. In technical call centers, metrics must be designed to measure the internal as well the external performance. Some of the metrics to consider may be call waiting time, dropped call, call routing time, quality of the service, service level, average time to resolve calls, and so on.

Defining the critical performance metrics is important. This must include establishing the customer requirements, identifying quantifiable process outputs and their measurement plan, and establishing targets against which the measured metrics will be compared.

2. *Analytics*: The types of analytics used are the core of BI program. These are qualitative, visualization, and quantitative models used to drive business decisions, find the optimal decisions through knowledge discovery and modeling. We explained the process, purpose, and tools of analytics earlier. They involve: visualization, data mining, process mining, statistical analysis, predictive analytics, predictive modeling including machine learning and artificial intelligence applications, business process modeling, and prescriptive analytics.

3. *Enterprise Reporting/Business Reporting* is a critical part of any organization. These are means and programs that provide infrastructure for strategic reporting to the management regarding the business. These reporting tools include data visualization, management information system, OLAP, and others.

4. *Collaboration/Collaboration Platform* program that connects both inside and outside of the company to exchange and use data through data sharing and electronic data interchange.

5. *Knowledge Management* program to make the company data-driven using strategies and practices that identify, create, distribute and manage the knowledge through learning management.

In addition to the aforementioned, BI can be designed to provide alert system and functionality with a capability to immediately warn the end-user if certain requirements are not met. For example, if certain critical business metric exceeds a pre-defined threshold, a warning may be issued using via e-mail or another monitoring service to alert the responsible person so that a corrective action may be taken. This is similar to automating the system to better manage and take timely actions.

Success Factors for BI Implementation

According to Kimball et al., there are three critical areas that organizations should assess before getting ready to do a BI project [25]:

1. The level of commitment and sponsorship of the project from senior management.
2. The level of business need for creating a BI implementation.
3. The amount and quality of business data available.

Comparing BI with Business Analytics

BI and BA are sometimes used interchangeably, but there are alternate definitions [26]. One definition contrasts the two, stating that the term BI refers to collecting business data to find information primarily through asking questions, reporting, and online analytical processes. BA, on the other hand, uses statistical and quantitative tools for explanatory and predictive modeling [27].

Viewed in this context, BA is a powerful and complex field that incorporates wide application areas including statistical analysis, predictive analytics, text and speech analytics, web analytics, visualization, causal analysis, decision processes and much more.

Business Analytics as Applied to Different Areas

Depending upon the application areas, analytics has different name. Some examples are:

Web analytics
Supply chain analytics
Marketing analytics
Human resource analytics
Financial analytics
Applications of analytics in other areas

Business Analytics and Business Intelligence

So what distinguishes BA from BI? Where does the BA fit in the scope of BI? Analytics is the science of analysis—the processes by which we interpret data, draw conclusions and make decisions. BA goes well beyond simply presenting data and creating visuals, crunching numbers, and computing statistics. The essence of analytics lies in the application—making sense from the data using prescribed methods, tools and logic to draw meaningful conclusion from the data. It uses logic and intelligence, and mental processes that enable us to reason, organize, plan, analyze, solve problems, understand, innovate, learn, and make decisions.

BA covers a vast area. It is a complex field that encompasses visualization, statistics and statistical modeling, statistical analysis, predictive analytics, text and speech analytics, web analytics, decision processes and much more.

BI combines a broad set of data analysis applications as mentioned earlier. It includes applications including querying, enterprise reporting, OLAP, mobile BI, real-time BI, operational BI, and cloud applications. BI technology also includes data visualization software for designing charts and other infographics, as well as tools for building BI dashboards and performance scorecards that display visualized data on business metrics and KPIs in an easy-to-grasp way. BI applications can be bought separately from different vendors or as part of a unified BI platform from a single vendor.

BI programs can also incorporate forms of advanced analytics, such as data mining, predictive analytics, text mining, statistical analysis, and big data analytics. In many cases advanced analytics projects are conducted and managed by separate teams of data scientists, statisticians, predictive modelers and other skilled analytics professionals, while BI teams oversee more straightforward querying and analysis of business data.

Difference Between Business Analytics (BA) Versus Business Intelligence (BI)

https://go.christiansteven.com/business-analytics-vs.-business-intelligence-heres-the-difference. BI and BA have somewhat similar goals. Both of these programs are about increasing the efficiency of the business by utilizing data analysis. The purpose of both BA and BI is to drive the business decisions based on the data. They exist to increase the efficiency and viability of a business and are data driven decision making approaches. Most businesses use the terms BI and BA interchangeably. If you really want to understand where people draw the line, there are different opinions.

There is no real consensus on exactly what constitutes BI and what constitutes BA, or where the lines are drawn. However, it seems logical to differentiate the two in the following way:

Business intelligence (BI)	Business analytics (BA)
BI is about accessing and analyzing *big data* using specialized big data software and infrastructure using powerful BI software specially designed to handle big data	BA is about predicting future trends using data analysis, statistics, statistical and quantitative modeling and analysis
BI is more concerned with the *whats* and the *hows* than the *whys*. Through data exploration it tries to answer the following questions: What happened? When? Who? How?	BA tries to answer the following questions: Why did something happen? Will it happen again? What will happen if we make changes to some of the inputs? What the data is telling us that we were not able to see before?

(Continued)

(Continued)

Business intelligence (BI)	Business analytics (BA)
BI looks into past or historical data to better understand the business performance. It is about improving performance and creating new strategic opportunities for growth	BA uses statistical analysis and predictive modeling to establish trends, figuring out why things are happening, and making an educated guess about how things will turn out in the future
Through data analysis, BI determines what has already occurred This insight is very helpful in process improvement efforts For example, through this analysis, you clearly see what is going well, but also learn to recover from what went wrong	BA primarily predicts what will happen in the future. It combines advanced statistical analysis and predictive modeling to give you an idea of what to expect so that you can anticipate developments or make changes now to improve outcomes
Tools of BI BI lets you apply chosen metrics to potentially huge, structured and unstructured datasets, and covers: querying, reporting, OLAP, analytics, data mining, process mining, business performance management, benchmarking, text mining, predictive analytics and prescriptive analytics BI tells you what happened, or what is happening right now in your business—it describes the situation to you. Not only that, a good BI platform describes this to you in real time in as much granular, forensic detail you need BI is the "descriptive" part of data analysis; whereas BA means BI plus the predictive element and all the extra bits and pieces that make up the way you handle, interpret and visualize data	BA is more about anticipated future trends of the KPIs. This is about using the past data and models to make predictions. This is different from the reporting in BI. Analytics models use the data with a view to drawing out new, useful insights to improve business planning and boost future performance. BA helps the company to meet the changes and then take advantage of coming developments. BA can be seen as a part of BI Tools of BA Statistics/statistical modeling Quantitative analysis Data mining Predictive modeling/analytics Text analytics Other types of analytics Prescriptive analytics and tools

Is there really a difference between *business analytics* and *business intelligence*? The answer is **Yes** and **No**.

Both BI and BA have similar objectives. They are data driven decision making programs. BI uses masses of raw data to learn about what is happening to the business. If you want to learn about the current state of the business through data analysis, reporting, application of big data software, descriptive statistics, data dashboards, and you are drawing conclusions and interpretation without extensively using predictive modeling tools, you will likely fall under BI, rather than BA.

Both approaches are valuable and critical to decision making in their own ways. It is important to know and understand whether your objective is descriptive analytics or you want to predict and optimize business outcomes. In the latter case, you will need predictive analysis, and prescriptive analytics. This understanding is critical before investing in such programs.

To summarize, BI is the "descriptive" part of data analysis; whereas, BA means BI, plus the predictive and prescriptive elements, plus all the visualization tools and extra bits and pieces that make up the way you handle, interpret visualize, and analyze data.

And lastly, there are those who say that there is hardly any distinction between the two. It does not matter what you call them as long as you can reach your goals. *There is no genuine difference between the two—or, if there is, it's not worth paying attention to. It seems like they do differ in the tools they use and how you use them to meet your objectives.*

Put simply, companies have always needed (and will always need) insights about their business performance for the same core reasons, but the skills, technologies, and strategies used to draw out those insights evolve all the time.

The tools of BA and BI depend upon whether your data requirements are geared more toward descriptive or predictive analytics to direct your business in the right direction—regardless of the terminology behind the tool.

https://sisense.com/blog/whats-the-difference-between-business-intelligence-and-business-analytics/

The potential benefits of BI and BA programs include accelerating and improving decision making; optimizing internal business processes; increasing operational efficiency; driving new revenues; and gaining competitive advantages over business rivals. BI systems can also help companies identify market trends and spot business problems that need to be addressed.

Summary

This chapter discussed BI and BA as decision making tools in businesses today. The chapter outlined the differences between the two and also the tools in each of these areas. The connection between BI and BA tools combined with the applications in the computer science and information technology are critical for the success of BA in a company. The chapter discussed the concepts of BI, BA, DA, and computer and information technology and how they are used in business decision making. The chapter also distinguishes between BI and BA, and the specific tools used in each case.

BI comprises of the processes, technologies, strategies, and analytical methods that turn the data or information into knowledge that are critical to driving business decisions. These tools, methods and technologies help companies in running business operations and making fact-based data driven decisions. In 1989, Howard Dresner (later a Gartner analyst) proposed "business intelligence" as an umbrella term to describe "concepts and methods to improve business decision making by using fact-based support systems."[28] It was not until the late 1990s that this usage became widespread [29].

The overall objectives of the BI and BA programs are similar. Companies are adopting these programs because these are critical in driving business decisions based on the current data. In a broad sense, BI incorporates the tools of BA including the descriptive, predictive, and prescriptive analytics that help companies in data-driven business decisions.

BI looks into past or historical data to better understand the business performance. It is about improving performance, and creating new strategic opportunities for growth. BA is more about anticipated future trends of the KPIs. This is about using the past data and models to make predictions. This is different from the reporting in BI. Analytics models use the data with a view to drawing out new, useful insights to improve business planning and boost future performance. BA primarily predicts what will happen in the future. It combines advanced statistical analysis and predictive and prescriptive modeling to give you an idea of what to expect so that you can anticipate developments or make changes now to improve outcomes. The specific tools of BA are all types of regression models, data mining, machine learning and more recently neural networks and deep learning.

Glossary of Terms Related to Business Intelligence

Business Intelligence Dashboard

http://searchbusinessanalytics.techtarget.com/definition/business -intelligence-dashboard

A BI dashboard is a data visualization tool that displays the current status of metrics and KPIs for an enterprise. Dashboards consolidate and arrange numbers, metrics and several of views of key business activities on one display. It also can display performance scorecards on a single screen. The essential features of a BI dashboard product include a customizable interface and the ability to pull real-time data from multiple sources.

Metric

A metric is the measurement of a particular characteristic of a company's performance or efficiency. Metrics are the variables whose measured values are tied to the performance of the organization. They are also known as the performance metrics because they are performance indicators.

Metrics may be finance based that focus on the performance of the organization. Some metrics are designed to measure requirements and value (customer wants and needs, what the customer wants, satisfaction level, and so on).

Key Performance Indicators (KPIs)

http://searchbusinessanalytics.techtarget.com/definition/key-performance-indicators-KPIs

KPIs are business *metrics* (measured key variables which are indicative of the performance of a company). These measurements are used by corporate executives and managers to track, analyze, and understand the factors that are critical to the success of an organization. Effective KPIs focus on the business processes and functions that senior management sees as most important for measuring progress toward meeting strategic goals and performance targets. The metrics provide opportunities for future improvement.

Data Warehouse

http://searchsqlserver.techtarget.com/definition/data-warehouse

A data warehouse is a repository for all the data that an enterprise collects from internal and external sources. It may contain data of different types.

The data are readily used for creating analytical and visual reports throughout the enterprise. Besides creating the reports, the stored data are used to model and perform analytics for the different operations in an enterprise including, sales, finance, marketing, engineering, and others. Before performing analyses on the data, cleansing, transformation, and data quality are critical issues. Typically, a data warehouse is housed on an enterprise mainframe server or increasingly, in the cloud. Data from various OLTP applications and various other sources is extracted for reporting, querying, and analytical applications.

The term data warehouse was coined by William H. Inmon, who is known as the Father of Data Warehousing. He described a data warehouse as being a subject-oriented, integrated, time-variant and *nonvolatile* collection of data that supports management's decision-making process.

Data Cleansing and Transformation

Data Cleansing or *data cleaning* is the process of detecting and correcting (or removing) corrupt or inaccurate records from a record set, table, or database and refers to identifying incomplete, incorrect, inaccurate or irrelevant data and then replacing, modifying, or deleting the corrupt data [30].

Data Transformation: In computing, *data transformation* is the process of converting data from one format or structure into another format or structure. It is a fundamental aspect of most data integration and data management tasks such as *data warehousing**, *data integration* and *application integration*. Data transformation can be simple or complex based on the required changes to the data between the source (initial) data and the target (final) data.

Data Quality

Data quality is about assuring and making the data ready for analysis. The data must meet certain criteria before it can be used for analysis.

Business Intelligence (BI)

BI looks into past or historical data to better understand the business performance. It is about improving performance, and creating new strategic opportunities for growth.

Business Analytics (BA)

BA is about predicting future trends using data analysis, statistical and quantitative modeling and analysis.

> **Descriptive Analytics**
> *Background Information: Data, Data Analysis, and Decision Making*

Overview: Descriptive Analytics

Descriptive analytics tools are used to understand the occurrence of certain business phenomenon or outcomes and explaining these outcomes through graphical, quantitative and numerical analysis. Through the visual and simple analysis, descriptive analytics explores the current performance of the business and the possible reasons for the occurrence of certain phenomenon. Many of the hidden patterns and features not apparent through mere examination of data can be exposed through graphical and numerical analysis. Descriptive analytics uses simple tools to uncover many of the problems quickly and easily. The results enable us question many of the outcomes so that corrective actions can be taken.

Successful use and implementation of descriptive analytics requires the understanding of data, types and sources of data, data preparation for analysis (data cleansing, transformation, and modeling), difference between unstructured and structured data, and data quality. Graphical/ visual representation of data, and graphical techniques using computer are basic requirements of descriptive analytics. These concepts related to data, data types including the graphical and visual techniques are explained in detail in Chapters 3 and 4. The visual techniques of descriptive analytics tools include the commonly used graphs and charts along with some newly developed graphical tools such as, bullet graphs, tree maps, and data dashboards. Dashboards are now becoming very popular with big data. They are used to display the multiple views of the business data graphically.

The other aspect of descriptive analytics is an understanding of simple numerical methods including the measures of central tendency, measures of position, measures of variation, and measures of shape, and how different measures and statistics are used to draw conclusions and make decision from the data. Some other topics of interest are the understanding of empirical rule and the relationship between two variables—the covariance, and correlation coefficient. The tools of descriptive analytics are helpful in understanding the data, identifying the trend or patterns in the data, and making sense from the data contained in the databases of companies. The understanding of databases, data warehouse, web search and query, and big data concepts are important in extracting and applying descriptive analytics tools. The following flow chart outlines the tools and methods used in descriptive analytics.

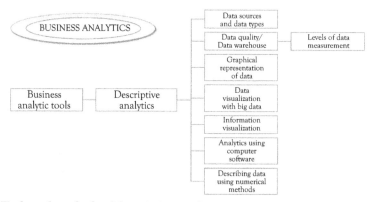

Tools and methods of descriptive analytics

PART II
Descriptive Analytics

CHAPTER 3

Data, Data Types, and Descriptive Statistics

Chapter Highlights

Making Sense from Data: Descriptive Statistics

Data and Data Analysis Concepts

    Statistics and Data at a Glance: What You Need to Know

    Current Developments in Data Analysis

Preparing Data for Analysis

    Data Cleansing, Data Transformation

    Data Warehouse

    Data, Data Types, and Data Quality

Statistics Defined

    Two Main Reasons for Studying Statistics

Statistics and Statistical Methods

    Descriptive and Inferential Statistics

Concept of Population and Sample

    Population and Sample Data

    Data and Classification of Data

    Qualitative (Categorical), Quantitative (Discrete and Continuous Data)

Data Types Data Collection

    Cross-Sectional data, Concept of Variables, Discrete, Continuous, and Time-Series Data

    Describing Data Using Levels of Measurement

    Types of Measurement Scale

        Nominal, Ordinal, Interval, and Ratio Scales

    Data Collection, Presentation, and Analysis

        How Data Are Collected: Sources of Data for Research and Analysis

Web as a Major Source of Data
Data Related Terms Applied to Analytics
Big Data, **Data mining,** Data Warehouse, **Structured versus Unstructured Data,** Data Quality

Making Sense from Data: Data and Data Analysis Concepts

Statistics and Data at a Glance: What You Need to Know

Statistics is the science and art of making decision using data. It is often called the science of data and is about analyzing and drawing meaningful conclusions from the data. Almost every field uses data and statistics to learn about systems and their processes. In fields such as business, research, health care, and engineering, a vast amount of raw data are collected and warehoused rapidly. This data must be analyzed to be meaningful. Data and statistical tools aid in gaining skills such as:

(1) Collecting, describing, analyzing, and interpreting data for intelligent decision-making (2) realizing that variation is an integral part of data and almost all data show variation (3) understanding the nature and pattern of variability of a phenomenon in the data, and (4) being able to measure reliability of the population parameters from which the sample data are collected to draw valid inferences.

The applications of statistics can be found in a majority of issues that concern everyday life. Examples include surveys related to consumer opinions, marketing studies, and economic and political polls.

Current Developments in Data Analysis

Because of the advancement in technology, it is now possible to collect massive amounts of data. Lots of data, such as web data, e-commerce, purchase transactions at retail stores, and bank and credit card transaction data, among more, is collected and warehoused by businesses. There has been an increasing amount of pressure on businesses to provide high quality products and services to improve their market share in this highly competitive market. Not only it is critical for businesses to meet and exceed customer needs and requirements, but it is also important for businesses to process and analyze a large amount of data efficiently in order to seek hidden patterns in the data. The processing and analysis of large data sets comes under the emerging field known as *big data* and *data mining*.

To process these massive amounts of data, data mining uses statistical techniques and algorithms and extracts non-trivial, implicit, previously unknown, and potentially useful patterns. Because applications of data mining tools are growing, there will be more of a demand for professionals trained in data mining. The knowledge discovered from this data in order to make intelligent data driven decisions is referred to as *business intelligence* and *business analytics*. *Business intelligence (BI)* is a hot topic in business and leadership circles today as it uses a set of techniques and processes which aid in fact-based decision making.

Preparing Data for Analysis

In statistical applications, data analysis may be viewed as the applications of *descriptive statistics*, *data visualization*, and *exploratory data analysis* (EDA). Before data can be analyzed, data preparation is important. Since the data are collected and obtained from different sources, a number of steps are necessary to assure data quality. These include *data cleaning* or *data cleansing*, *data transformation*, *modeling*, *data warehousing*, and maintaining *data quality*.

Requirements of Data Analysis:

Data analytics involves *cleansing*, organizing, presenting, *transforming*, and *modeling data* to gain insight and discover useful information. These are prerequisites to data analytics and are explained in the following.

One of the most important requirements and criteria of data analytics is *data quality*. The purpose is drawing meaningful conclusions and making data driven decisions. Data analysis has different forms and approaches, and it uses different techniques depending upon the objectives. BI uses data analysis applications that focus on business information.

There are other forms of data analysis techniques with advanced applications. For example, *Data Mining* is also a data analysis technique with an objective of knowledge discovery from the data for predictive purposes. In statistical applications, data analysis may be viewed as the applications of *descriptive statistics*, *data visualization*, and *exploratory data analysis* (EDA).

Prerequisites to Data Analytics: Data Preparation for Data Analytics

Before the data can be used effectively for analysis, the following some data preparation steps are essential. These are:

1. Data cleansing;
2. Scripting;
3. Data transformation; and
4. Data warehousing.

Data cleansing or *data cleaning* is the process of detecting and correcting (or removing) corrupt or inaccurate records from a record set, table, or database and refers to identifying incomplete, incorrect, inaccurate or irrelevant data and then replacing, modifying, or deleting the corrupt data [31]. Data cleansing may be performed interactively with *data wrangling* which is transforming and mapping data from one format to the other usually from the "*raw*" data to the other data format to make the data more appropriate for processing and analytics applications. Often *scripting* is also used in data cleaning and transformation.

A *scripting* or *script language* is a programming language that supports *scripts*: programs used to automate or execute the tasks that could alternatively be executed one-by-one by a human operator. Scripting languages have applications in automating software applications, web pages in a web browser, operating systems (OS), embedded systems, and games. After cleansing, a data set should be consistent with other similar data sets in the system and suitable for further analysis. [https://en.wikipedia.org/wiki/Data_cleansing]

Data transformation: In computing, *data transformation* is the process of converting data from one format or structure into another format or structure. It is a fundamental aspect of most data integration and data management tasks such as *data warehousing**, *data integration*, and application integration. *Data transformation* can be simple or complex based on the required changes to the data between the source (initial) data and the target (final) data. [https://en.wikipedia.org/wiki/Data_transformation]

Data Warehousing

A data warehouse (*DW* or *DWH*), or *enterprise data warehouse* (*EDW*), is a system for storing, reporting, and analyzing huge amounts of data. The purpose of DW is creating reports and performing analytics which are core component of *Business Intelligence*. DWs are central repositories used to store and integrate current and historical data from one or many sources. The data readily available are used for creating analytical and visual reports throughout the enterprise. The data stored in the warehouse may be used for creating reports and performing analytics for the different operations in an enterprise including, sales, finance, marketing, engineering, and others. Before performing analyzes on the data, cleansing, transformation, and data quality are critical issues. We describe data quality later in this section.

Data and Data Quality

In data analysis and analytics, data can be viewed as *information*. Data are also *measurements*. The purpose of data analysis is to make sense from data. Data when collected (in its raw form) is known as *raw data*. These are the data not processed.

In data analysis, data needs to be converted into a form suitable for reporting and analytics. [http://searchdatamanagement.techtarget.com/definition/data]

It is acceptable for data to be used as a singular subject or a plural subject. *Raw data* is a term used to describe data in its most basic digital format.

Data Quality

Data quality is crucial to the reliability and success of business analytics (BA) and BI programs. Both the analytics and BI are data driven programs.

Analytics is about analyzing data to drive business decisions; whereas BI is about reporting.

Data quality is affected by the way data is collected, entered in the system, stored and managed. Efficient and accurate storage (data warehouse), cleansing, and data transformation are critical for assuring data quality. The process of verifying the reliability and effectiveness of data is sometimes referred to as data quality assurance (DQA). The effectiveness, reliability, and success of BA and BI depend on the acceptable data quality.

The following are important considerations in assuring data quality. Aspects of data quality include: [http://searchdatamanagement.techtarget.com/definition/data-quality]

Accuracy
Completeness
Update status
Relevance
Consistency across data sources
Reliability
Appropriate presentation
Accessibility

Within an organization, acceptable data quality is crucial to operational and transactional processes.

Maintaining data quality requires going through the data periodically and scrubbing it. Typically, this involves updating and standardizing the data, and de-duplicating records to create a single view of the data, even if it is stored in multiple disparate systems. There are many vendor applications in the market to make this job easier.

Data Analysis: Advanced Applications: There are other forms of data analysis techniques with advanced applications. For example, *Data Mining* is also a data analysis technique with an objective of knowledge discovery from the data for predictive purposes. In statistical applications, data analysis may be viewed as the applications of *descriptive statistics*, *data visualization*, inferential statistics techniques, and *exploratory data analysis* (EDA), and statistical modeling.

Since the field of statistics and data analysis is synonymous, we introduce statistics.

Statistics Defined

Some definitions of statistics are given as follows:

1. Statistics is about making decisions from data.
2. Statistics is a science that deals with collection, tabulation, analysis, interpretation, and presentation of data (in order to make decisions).
3. Statistics is the science concerned with problems involving chance variations that result from a large number of small and independent influences operating on each measured result.
4. Statistics is concerned with making decisions from data involving chance variations.
5. Statistics deals with making inferences or predictions about a population based on sample data.

Two Main Reasons for Studying Statistics

There are two main characteristics that make the study of statistics important.

1. Statistics is the branch of mathematics that deals with variation and is often called mathematics of variation. Most of the data we collect show variation and an element (such as, a person, thing, or event) upon which we collect data can be seen as a *variable*. *A variable is a characteristic of interest that differs among observations or measurements.* We can study the variation in data using statistics. Statistical thinking and variation reduction are major goals in data analysis, decision making, and quality improvement programs such as Six Sigma.
2. Statistical methods enable us to draw conclusions using limited data, or it enables us to draw conclusion about a population using the sample data. For example, we can estimate the average height of women in a county without actually measuring the height of all of them.

Statistics and Statistical Methods

Statistics and statistical methods are used in collecting, presenting, and analyzing data. Subsequent chapters will discuss the process of collecting and analyzing data, describing data using charts and graphs, or creating visual representation of data, and the tools for analyzing and interpreting data so that meaningful conclusions can be drawn and effective decisions can be made.

Statistics deals with variation. All data show variation and statistics is the tool that deals with variation in the data. Statistical tools and techniques allow us to study the variation in the data. Variation is a part of any process or system and it must be kept within certain limit for any process to work efficiently. Analyzing and reducing variation is the major goal of many companies using quality control programs such as, six-sigma and lean six-sigma. The topics in here will help you understand the concepts of statistics and data analysis, variation, and introduce you to the tools and techniques used in analyzing data from businesses and other processes. Use of computer software in analyzing data is emphasized throughout this text.

Statistics is studied under two broad categories: *descriptive statistics* and *inferential statistics. Descriptive statistics* uses graphical and numerical methods to describe and analyze data. *Inferential statistics or inference procedures* are part of statistics concerned with drawing conclusions about the *population* using *sample data.*

Population denotes the entire measurements that are theoretically possible. It is also known as the universe and is the totality of items or things under consideration. For example, total number of light bulbs manufactured by a company in a given period of time, or number of people who can vote in a country, and so on.

Sample is the portion of the population that is selected for analysis (a subset of population).

A population is described by its *parameter;* whereas, a sample is described by its *statistics.*

A parameter is a summary measure that is computed to describe the characteristic of a population. *A statistic* is a summary measure that is computed to describe the characteristic of a sample.

Table 3.1 Population parameters and sample statistics

Population parameters
N: *the population size*
μ: *the population mean*
σ^2: *the population variance*
σ: *the population standard deviation*
p: *the population proportion*
Sample statistics
The corresponding sample statistics are denoted using the symbols below.
n: *the sample size*
$\bar{x}$: *the sample mean*
s^2: *the sample variance*
s: *the sample standard deviation*
$\bar{p}$: *the sample proportion*

Table 3.1 summarizes the population parameters and the sample statistics, and the symbols used to describe them.

The population mean is denoted using the Greek symbol μ (read as "mu"), *population variance σ^2* (read as sigma-squared), the *population standard deviation is denoted using another Greek symbol σ* (σ read as "sigma"), and the *population proportion is denoted by, p.* Note that each parameter is denoted using a specific symbol.

The sample statistics are the *sample mean, $\bar{x}$* (read as "x-bar"), *sample variance, s^2, sample standard deviation, s, sample median,* and *sample proportion, $\bar{p}$* (read as p-bar). It is important to know the distinction between the population parameters and the sample statistics and the way they are described.

Statistical inference involves generalization and a statement about the reliability or probability of its validity. For example, an engineer or a scientist can make inferences about a population by analyzing the samples. Decisions can then be made based on the sample results. Making decisions or drawing conclusions using sample data raises question about the likelihood of the decisions being correct. This helps us understand why probability theory is used in statistical analysis.

Using probability models, we can apply the probability approach to estimate the population parameters. The choice of the proper probability distribution to represent any given data comes with experience and knowledge of statistical theory. By using certain statistical hypothesis, we test the correctness of the probability distribution.

Data and Classification of Data

Data are any number of related observations. We collect data to draw conclusions or to make decisions. Data often provide the *basis* for decision-making.

A single data or observation is known as a *data point.* A collection of data is a *data set.* In statistics, reference to data means a collection of data or a data set.

Data can also be *qualitative* or *quantitative. Quantitative data* are numerical data that can be expressed in numbers. For example, data collected on temperature, sales and demand, length, height, and volume are all examples of quantitative data.

Qualitative data are data for which the measurement scale is categorical. Qualitative data are also known as *categorical data.* Examples of qualitative data include the color of your car, response to a yes/no question, or the product rating using a Likert scale of 1 to 5 where the numbers correspond to a category (excellent, good, and so on).

Data can also be classified as *time series data* or *cross-sectional data. Time series* data are the data recorded over time; for example, weekly sales, monthly demand for a product, or the number of orders received by an online shopping department of a department store.

Cross-sectional data are the values observed at the same point in time. For example, the closing value of the stock market on the 5th of each month for the past 12 months would be considered cross-sectional because all observations correspond to one point in time.

Statistical techniques are more suited to quantitative data. These techniques involve principles and methods used in collecting and analyzing data.

Data Elements are the entities—the specific items—that we are collecting data about. For example, data collected on the stock price for the following companies:

Company	Stock price ($)
Coca Cola	44
Facebook	173
Microsoft	90
Amazon	1525
Micron	60

Each company's stock price is an **element**. Thus, there are five elements in this data set.

Variable: In statistics, a variable can be thought of as an object upon which the data are collected. This object can be a person, entity, thing, or an event. The stock price of the aforementioned companies is a *variable*. Note that stock values show variation. In case of stock prices for previously mentioned companies, we can say that the stock price is a variable because the prices vary. If data are collected on daily temperature for a month, the temperature will show variation. Thus, the temperature is a *variable*. Similarly, data collected on sales, profit, the number of customers served by a bank, the diameter of a shaft produced by a manufacturing company, the number of housing starts; all show variation therefore, these are *variables*. Using statistics, we can study the variation. A variable is generally a characteristic of interest in the data. A data set may contain one or more variables of interest. For example, we showed the stock price of five companies in the previous example. There is only one variable in the data: the stock price. If we also collected data on earnings and P/E (price to earnings) ratio of each company, we would have three variables.

Another Classification of Data

Data are also classified as:

- *Discrete*, or
- *Continuous*

Discrete data are the result of a counting process. These are expressed as whole numbers or integers. Some examples of discrete data are cars sold by Toyota in the last quarter, the number of houses sold last year, or the number of defective parts produced by a company. All these are expressed in whole numbers and are examples of discrete data.

Continuous data can take any value within a given range. These are measured on a continuum or a scale that can be divided infinitely. More powerful statistical tools are available to deal with continuous data as compared to discrete data; therefore, continuous data are preferred wherever possible. Some examples of continuous data include measurements of length, height, diameter, temperature, stock value, sales, and so on. Discrete and continuous data may also be referred as *discrete* and *continuous variables.*

Data Types and Data Collection

Data are often collected on a variable of interest. For example, we may collect data on the stock value of a particular technology stock, number of jobs created in a month, or diameters of a shaft manufactured by a manufacturing company. In all these cases the data will vary, for example, the diameter measurement will vary from shaft to shaft. Data can also be collected using a survey where a questionnaire is designed for data collection purposes. The response in a survey generally varies from person to person. In other words, the response obtained is *random*.

In the data collection process, the response or the measurements may be *qualitative, quantitative, discrete* or *continuous*. If the data are quantitative they can be either discrete or continuous. Thus, the data can be classified as:

- *Qualitative data,* and
- *Quantitative data*

This classification of data is shown in Figure 3.1.

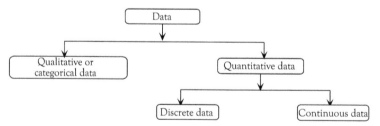

Figure 3.1 Classification of quantitative data

Describing Data Using the Levels of Measurement

Data are also described according to the *levels of measurement* used. In the broadest sense, all collected data are *measured* in some form. Even the discrete quantitative data are nothing but *measurement through counting*.

Types of Measurement Scales

There are four levels of measurements:

1. Nominal Scale
2. Ordinal Scale
3. Interval Scale
4. Ratio Scale

The nominal is the weakest and ratio is the strongest form of measurement.

Nominal and Ordinal Scales

Data obtained from a qualitative variable are measured on a *nominal scale* or *ordinal scale*. If the observed data are classified into various distinct categories in which *no ordering* is implied, a *nominal level* of measurement is achieved. See the following examples.

Qualitative Variable Category

Marital status   Married   Single
Stock ownership   Yes   No
Political party affiliation Democrat Republican Independent
If the observed data are classified into distinct categories in which ordering is implied, an *ordinal level* of measurement is obtained.

Qualitative variable Ordered categories

Student grades   A B C D F
Rank of employees   Senior engineer, Engineer, and Engineer trainee
Product quality   Excellent, good, poor (highest to lowest)

Nominal scale is the weakest form of measurement. Ordinal scale is also a weak form of measurement because no meaningful numerical statements can be made about the different categories. For example: the ordinal scale only tells which category is greater, but does not tell how much greater.

Interval and Ratio Scales

Interval Scale: These measurements are made on a quantitative scale. It is an ordered scale in which the difference between any two measurements is a meaningful quantity. For example, a person who is 70 inches tall is 2 inches taller than someone who is 68 inches tall. The difference of 2 inches would also be obtained if the heights of two persons were 78 and 76 inches. The difference has the same meaning anywhere on the scale. Some examples are:

Quantitative Variable Levels of Measurement
Temperature interval
Time interval

Ratio Scale: If in addition to the difference being meaningful and equal at all points on a scale, there is also a "true zero" point in which the ratio of measurements are sensible to consider, then the scale is a ratio scale. The measurements are made from the same reference point. For example, a measurement of 80 inches in length is twice as long as a measurement of 40 inches. Measurements of length are ratio scale. Examples of ratio scale are:

Quantitative Variable Level of Measurements

Height (in feet, inches) ratio
Weight (in pounds, kilograms) ratio
Age (in years, days) ratio
Salary (in dollars) ratio

Data obtained from a quantitative variable are measured on an interval or a ratio scale. Ratio is the highest level of measurement. It tells which observed value is largest, and by how much. Figure 3.2 shows the classification of data according to the levels of measurements.

Data Collection, Presentation, and Analysis

In this section, we describe:

- How data are collected (obtained) and prepared for statistical analysis

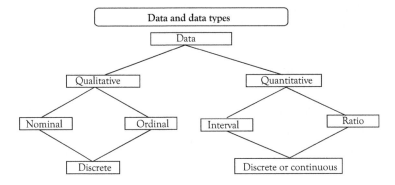

Figure 3.2 Classifications of data

- Tabular presentation of data
- Graphical presentation of data
- Analysis and interpretation of data

In statistical analysis, we always encounter situations where we need to draw conclusion from the data. Effective decision-making requires information. For the statistician or researcher, the information needed to make effective decisions is in the data. For a statistical analysis to be useful, and to make an effective decision, the input data must be appropriate. If the data are insufficient, flawed, ambiguous, or have errors, even the most sophisticated statistical tools will not provide meaningful results.

How Data Are Collected:
Sources of Data for Research and Analysis

Web as a Major Source of Data

Data can be obtained from industrial, individual, or government sources. The Internet is now one of the major sources of data. A number of website can be accessed using search engines like Google to obtain data. There are a number of websites that collect data on employment, consumer price index, population, housing, and manufacturing. Law enforcement agencies collect data on crimes. A great deal of business and economic data can be obtained from the web sites of Bureau of Economic Analysis (BEA), the Bureau of Labor Statistics (BLS), the U.S. Census Bureau, the

Federal Reserve Economic Data (FRED), and the National Association of Manufacturers (NAM). Besides these, a vast amount of data on current issues, stock markets, economics, sports and other areas of interest can be obtained from the websites of reputable publications including *USA Today, The Wall Street Journal,* The *Economist, Money Magazine, The New York Times,* to name a few. Table 3.2 provides a list of some Internet sites and data that can be obtained from these sites.

Other sources from where data can be obtained or collected are:

- ***Government agencies not listed earlier:*** Government agencies collect data on travel, health care, economic measures, unemployment, interest rates, and so on.
- ***Experimental design:*** An experiment is any process that generates data. Design of experiment involves changing the values

Table 3.2 Selected Internet sites and available data

Internet site	Available data
Bureau of Labor Statistics (www.bls.gov)	Principal fact-finding agency for the Federal Government in the broad field of labor economics and statistics. Information on jobs, salary, economic analysis, unemployment rates, occupational outlook, inflation rates, and more
U.S. Census Bureau (www.census.gov)	Principal agency of the U.S. Federal Statistical System, responsible for producing data about the American people and economy
Zillow.com	Real Estate data, data on home sales, rent, buy, home values, mortgage rates
www.cnbc.com	Latest business news on stock markets, financial & earnings on CNBC. View world markets streaming charts & video; check stock tickers and quotes
Finance.yahoo.com	Stock quotes, up to date news, stock prices, portfolio management resources, international market data, message boards, and mortgage rates
The Wall Street Journal, The New York Times, Money Magazine, Fortune	Data on finance, taxes, mortgage rate, retirement and other general interest
Bureau of Economic Analysis (BEA)	Source of U.S. economic statistics including national income and product accounts (NIPAs), consumer price index, gross domestic product (GDP), international data on trade

of input variables and observing their effect on the output or response variable of interest. The process provides useful data that can be used to optimize or troubleshoot a system.

- *Telephone/mail surveys*: Data can be obtained using telephone or mail surveys. Telephone surveys are inexpensive and very commonly used data collection method. The drawback is that it may generate low response rate as people may refuse to take part in the survey. The data collection method using mail questionnaire usually has the lowest response rate.
- *Processes*: Data are also collected from processes including manufacturing and service systems and processes. Data may directly be obtained from the process or experiments may be designed to obtain the needed information.

Besides the mail survey, data are also collected using other means of survey such as, telephone survey, door-to-door survey, and online survey using computer and Internet. In case where the data are collected using a survey, one should be careful in designing survey questionnaire. The questions should be concise, unambiguous and should convey the same meaning to everyone so that precise response can be generated. The response from the survey questions should meet the data collection objective. Whenever possible *closed-end questions* as opposed to *open-end questions* should be designed as the closed-end questions can be answered by selecting response from a short list of choices. In case of open-ended questions, the respondents do not have definite choices and these questions allow the freedom to respond using statements of their own choice. The response generated from open-ended questions sometimes may be difficult to compile for meaningful analysis. It may lack the *operational definition* which means that the questions and variables in the question may not convey the same meaning to everyone.

Analyzing Data Using Different Tools

The data when collected are in usually referred to raw data. Raw data are not analyzed. There is always goal or objective behind collecting data. The raw data must be processed and analyzed to make sense. A number of software including the big data software are now available that have the capability of handling small to massive amounts of data. In the chapters that follow we will continue our discussion on the following applications:

Visual representation of data

Graphical techniques using Excel

Graphical techniques using popular software packages

Computer applications and implementation

Data Related Terms Applied to Analytics

Big Data

Big Data is a collection of data sets so large and complex that it becomes difficult to process using on-hand database management tools or traditional data processing application [Wikipedia].

As per *O'Reilly media*

Big data is data that exceeds the processing capacity of conventional database systems. The data is too big, moves too fast, or doesn't fit the structures of your database architectures. To gain value from this data, you must choose an alternative way to process it. **O'Reilly Media** made Big Data popular.

Gartner who was credited with the 3 'V's of Big Data classified the big data as:

High-volume, high-velocity and/or high-variety information assets that demand cost-effective, innovative forms of information processing that enable enhanced insight, decision making, and process automation.

Gartner is referring to the size of data (large volume), speed with which the data is being generated (velocity), and the different types of data (variety) and this seemed to align with the combined definition of Wikipedia and O'Reilly media.

According to *Mike Gualtieri of Forrester*, the 3 'V's mentioned by Gartner are just measures of data. Mike insisted that Forrester's definition is more actionable. And that definition is:

Big Data is the frontier of a firm's ability to store, process, and access (SPA) all the data it needs to operate effectively, make decisions, reduce risks, and serve customers.

Data mining: Data mining is about finding meaningful patterns and deriving insights in large sets of data using sophisticated pattern recognition techniques. It is closely related to analytics that we discussed earlier. In data mining you mine the data to get analytics. To derive meaningful patterns, data miners use statistics and statistical modeling, machine learning algorithms, and artificial intelligence.

Data Warehouse

A data warehouse (DW or DWH), or *enterprise data warehouse* (EDW), is a system for storing, reporting, and analysis of huge amounts of data. The purpose of DW is creating reports and performing analytics which are core component of *Business Intelligence.* DWs are central repositories used to store and integrate current and historical data from one or many sources. The data are readily available and are used for creating analytical and visual reports throughout the enterprise. The data stored in the warehouse may be used for creating reports and performing analytics for the different operations in an enterprise including, sales, finance, marketing, engineering, and others. Before performing analyzes on the data; cleansing, transformation, and data quality are critical issues.

Structured versus Unstructured Data: are the "Volume" and "Variety" —the 'V's of Big Data. Structured data is the data that can be stored in the relational databases. This type of data can be analyzed and organized in such a way that can be related to other data via tables. Unstructured data cannot be directly put in the data bases or analyzed or organized directly. Some examples are e-mail/text messages, social media posts and recorded human speech, and so on.

Data Quality

Data quality is affected by the way data is collected, entered in the system, stored, and managed. Efficient and accurate storage (data warehouse), cleansing, and data transformation are critical for assuring data quality. The process of verifying the reliability and effectiveness of data is sometimes referred to as DQA. The effectiveness, reliability, and success of BA and BI depend on the acceptable data quality.

The following are important considerations in assuring data quality

Aspects of data quality include: [http://searchdatamanagement.techtarget.com/definition/data-quality]

- Accuracy
- Completeness
- Update status
- Relevance
- Consistency across data sources
- Reliability
- Appropriate presentation
- Accessibility

Within an organization, acceptable data quality is crucial to operational and transactional processes.

Summary

This chapter provided the basic concepts of data, types of data, statistics and statistical methods, two broad categories under which statistics is studied—descriptive and inferential statistics. Different types of data used in analyzes were explained along with the scales on which data are measured. These scales make the data weak or strong. Finally, the data collection steps, and sources of data were discussed. The data related terms as applied to analytics were outlined. Since analytics is all about analyzing data using different types of models, a clear understanding of data is critical.

CHAPTER 4

Descriptive Analytics: Data Visualization

Chapter Highlights

Introduction

Basic Concepts in Data Visualization

Presenting Data: Collection and Presentation of Data

      Organizing Data: An Example

Summarizing Quantitative Data: Frequency Distribution

      Histogram: A Graph of Frequency Distribution

      Example: Histogram: Summarizing Data and Examining the Distribution

Graphical Summary of Data

Graphical Display of Variation

Data visualization: Conventional and Simple Techniques

      Stem-and-Leaf Plot

      Box Plots

      More Applications of Box Plots

      Dot Plots

      Bar Charts, a Cluster Bar Chart, and Stacked Bar Chart

Describing, Summarizing, and Graphing Categorical Variables

      Creating Bar Chart from a Simple Tally

Example: Cross Tabulation with Two and Three Categorical Variables

      Pie Charts

Interval Plots

      Example: Interval Plot Showing the Variation in Sample Data

Time Series Plots

Sequence Plot: Plot of Process Data

      Example: Sequence Plot

Connected Line Plot
Area Graph
Summary of Widely Used Charts and Graphs
Measures of Association Between Two Quantitative Variables:
    Scatter Plot and the Coefficient of Correlation: Examples
Scatter Plot Showing a Non-linear Relationships Between x and y
Examples of Coefficient of Correlation
Exploring the Relationship Between Three Variables: Bubble Plot
    Additional Examples of Bubble Plots
Summary of Charts and Graphs Involving Scatter Plots, Bubble Plots, and Matrix Plots

Introduction

Data visualization is presenting the data visually or graphically. The graphical displays are extremely helpful in detecting the patterns, trends, and correlations that are not usually apparent from the raw data. The trends and the patterns in the data cannot be recognized and they go undetected if not in the visual form.

Data visualization is an integral part of business intelligence (BI). Most of the BI application software heavily emphasize on data visualization and have strong data visualization capabilities. One of the reasons for the popularity of visualization tools is that they are easier to use and comprehend and do not require extensive training as in the case of statistical software. A number of popular statistical software are available that heavily emphasize on analysis and modeling along with graphing capabilities. They are typically easier to operate than traditional statistical analysis software or earlier versions of BI software. This has led to a rise in lines of business implementing data visualization tools on their own, without support from IT.

The data visualization tools and software now have advanced capabilities. They go beyond the standard charts and graphs used in Microsoft Excel and other standard statistical software. Current data visualization software can display data in form of graphs and charts contained in dashboards that display multiple views of data. These dashboards are extremely helpful decision making tools. A number of specialized graphs including infographics, heat maps, geographic maps, detailed bar, and pie charts can be created using visualization software. In many cases, the visuals created may have interactive capabilities that allow for manipulating data, querying, and analysis.

Data visualization software plays an important role in big data and advanced analytics projects. Massive amounts of data are now collected by businesses. The visualization and analysis of this data is referred to as *big data* analysis. Visualization of big data requires specially designed software to quickly and easily get an overview through data dashboards.

The success of the two leading software vendors—Tableau and Qlik—has moved other vendors toward a more visual approach in their software. Virtually all big data software in the BI space has strong data visualization functionality. It does not mean that only the software designed for big data, such as Tableau and Qlik (the two leading vendors in the BI space) can only be used for data visualization. A number of standard statistical software including MINITAB, SAS, STATS PRO, SPSS, and others along with widely used spreadsheet program Excel are widely used for data visualization. The basics and fundamentals of visuals and graphics created using the standard statistical software or big data software are the same. The difference lies in their capabilities. Big data visualization software has capabilities of handling massive amounts of data. They are capable of creating *dashboards* that can provide multiple views of data on one plot. In this chapter, we provide the fundamentals of data visualization along with a number of examples of visuals that can be created from the data. We also provide the applications and interpretation of these visuals.

Basic Concepts in Data Visualization

One of the major functions of data analysis is to describe the data in a way that is easy to comprehend and communicate. This can be done both by presenting the data in graphical form and by calculating various summary statistics; such as, the measures of central tendency and the measures of variability. The graphical techniques enable the analyst to describe a data set that is more concise than the original data. These techniques help reveal the essential characteristics of the data so that effective decisions can be made.

In this chapter, we have presented numerous graphical techniques using standard computer software. The visualization using big data is the topic of the next chapter. You may be familiar with many of the commonly used charts and graphs; therefore, we will not discuss the theory behind them in detail. Instead, we will explain how to construct these graphs and charts using the computer and explain their important characteristics.

Presenting Data: Collection and Presentation of Data

In the previous chapter, we discussed the concepts and types of data. This chapter deals with applications. Following two methods are commonly used for describing data:

- **Tables, and**
- **Graphs**

The purpose of collecting data is to draw conclusions or to make decisions. To draw meaningful conclusion, the data are organized, grouped, plotted, and analyzed. Organizing data into groups is known as frequency *distribution. The data should represent all relevant groups.* Suppose a market survey is conducted to forecast the demand for a product in a particular area and 200 consumers are surveyed. It is important that this group contain a variety of consumers representing variables such as income level, education, gender, race, and so on.

Data can be collected through actual measurements or observations or can be obtained from government or company records. This information can be organized in a way that can be used to make decisions or draw conclusions. When data are arranged in a compact, usable form, decision makers can obtain reliable information and use it to make decisions.

Arrangement and display of data are important elements of descriptive statistics. Without some arranging, shifting, sorting, and grouping of the original data, we would not be able to arrive at a conclusion. Also, we need sufficient data to draw valid and meaningful conclusions. Decisions made from insufficient data may be misleading and incorrect.

Organizing Data: An Example

Initially when the data are collected, they are unorganized and in raw form that do not convey much meaning. The raw data must be organized in certain ways to be meaningful. Here, we provide an example on how data can be arranged and organized before analysis can be performed.

Table 4.1 shows the speed of 100 cars in miles per hour (mph) passing through a highway intersection with a 60 mph speed limit. These cars were randomly selected and represent a sample of $n=100$.

The data of Table 4.1 are called *raw data* (data which are not arranged and analyzed). The speeds of the cars were recorded in the order in which they occurred. This is *ungrouped data*. Ungrouped data enable us to study the sequence of values; for example, "low" or "high" values. The data may also be helpful in determining some causes of variation. However, for a large data set, the ungrouped data do not provide much information.

Table 4.2 shows the data of Table 4.1 ranked in increasing order of magnitude; that is, in *rank order*. This is also known as *data array* or *ordered array*. A data array arranges the values in increasing or decreasing order.

Table 4.1 Driving speed (mph)

51	46	62	70	54	59	59	57	61	66	49	57	57	65	61	62	51	63	62	65	55	55	65
64	60	55	70	61	63	55	70	65	51	53	49	62	56	61	64	54	60	63	69	72	69	60
57	63	60	56	60	61	57	57	61	54	58	55	69	63	55	58	58	62	59	59	62	53	69
56	59	57	60	63	60	56	52	65	58	60	62	54	57	60	53	56	60	71	59	64	58	71
68	62	61	61	67	59	58	49															

Table 4.2 Driving speed (mph)—(Sorted data)

46	49	49	49	51	51	51	52	53	53	53	54	54	54	54	55	55	55	55	55	55	56	56
56	56	56	57	57	57	57	57	57	57	57	58	58	58	58	58	58	59	59	59	59	59	59
59	60	60	60	60	60	60	60	60	60	60	61	61	61	61	61	61	61	61	62	62	62	62
62	62	62	62	63	63	63	63	63	63	64	64	64	65	65	65	65	65	66	67	68	69	69
69	69	70	70	70	71	71	72															

Summarizing Quantitative Data: Frequency Distribution

A *frequency distribution* provides a compact representation of data. This is also known as grouping. Compact representation is obtained by arranging the data into groups or *class intervals* usually of *equal width* and then recording or counting the number of observations in each interval. Counting the number of observations in each group is called the *class frequency*. For example, examine the data in Table 4.2. We can divide this data into 10 class intervals with a width of 3 and tabulate the results as shown in the following.

Class-Interval Frequency

Class- interval	Frequency
45–48	1
48–51	4
51–54	9
..... and so on.	

The aforementioned class frequency is an example of a frequency distribution. The class interval of 45–48 means that this interval contains all the values from 45 to 48 (not including 48). If we count the number of observations between 45 and 48 in Table 4.2; we will find there is one observation in this group. The count of 1 is known as the frequency. The class interval can also be written in a formal way as:

$$45 \leq X < 48$$

This means that the values in this class interval include the value 45 but not 48. The value 45 is known as the *lower class boundary or lower class limit* and the value 48 is known as the *upper class boundary or upper class limit*.

There are several other possibilities of grouping or constructing frequency distributions using the information in Table 4.2. The following information is helpful while grouping or forming a frequency distribution:

- When dividing the data into class intervals, 5–15 class intervals are recommended. If there are *too many class intervals*, the class frequency (count) is low and the savings in computational effort is small. If there are too few class intervals, the true characteristic of the distribution may be obscured and some information may be lost.

- The *number of class intervals* should be governed by the *amount* and *scatter* of data present.

Forming *Frequency Distribution or Grouping* the data in Table 4.2.

- For the data in Table 4.2, approximate number of classes can be found using the formula: $K = 1 + 3.33 \log_{10}$ where K is the number of classes and n is the number of observations. Using this formula, the number of class-intervals was found to be 7.66 or 8. Note that the value obtained using this formula is approximate. We may decide to divide the data into 10 class intervals. The next step is to find the *width* of the class or *class-width*.

- Note that the number of observations in Table 4.2 is $n = 100$ and we decide to divide the data into $K =$ number of classes=10. Using these values, the class width using the following equation:

$$\text{Class width} = \frac{72 - 46}{10} = 2.6$$

This width is also approximate. We may choose to have a width of 3.0 rather than 2.6. From the data in Table 4.2, suppose we decided to divide the data into 10 class intervals with a class-width of 3.0. Using a class width of 3.0, the frequency distribution is shown in Table 4.3. The second column contains the frequency or the number of observations in each class. This is obtained by sorting the data from the lowest to the highest number (as seen in Table 4.2) and counting the number of observations in each class. The interval 45–48 is read as 45 but less than 48. This means that the upper class boundary is exclusive. The class boundaries can also be formed with the upper boundary *inclusive*. In that case the class interval would be 45–47. In general, there should be *no gap* and *no overlap* between the class intervals. ***Note:*** For a given set of data, there is no one unique frequency distribution. Several frequency distributions are

Table 4.3 Frequency distribution of 100 drivers with 60 miles per hour (mph) speed limit

Class-interval (mph)	Frequency (f)
45–48	1
48–51	3
51–54	7
54–57	15
57–60	21
60–63	26
63–66	14
66–69	3
69–72	9
72–75	1
Total	$\sum f_i = 100$

possible for the same set of data. The grouping can be performed easily using many statistical software.

Histogram: A Graph of Frequency Distribution

A *histogram* is a graph used to illustrate the frequency distribution in a graphical form as shown in Figure 4.1. This graph is useful because it shows the pattern that is not so obvious when the data are in a table form. The histogram is also useful as it summarizes a large set of data. It is also useful in the study of probability distributions.

In a histogram, the class intervals are plotted on the horizontal axis and the frequencies are plotted on the vertical axis. The histogram is a series of rectangles, each proportional in width to the range of values within each class and is also proportional in height to the number of observations falling within each class.

Example 4.1 Histogram: Summarizing the Data and Examining the Distribution

The selling price of 300 homes for the past six months in a certain city is summarized in Figure 4.2 in form of a histogram. The bars show the

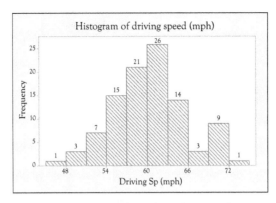

Figure 4.1 Histogram of driving speed (mph) (10 class-intervals)

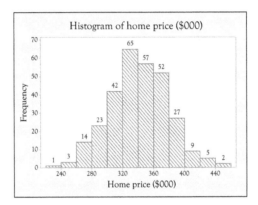

Figure 4.2 Histogram of home price ($000)

intervals of $20,000. The first class-interval of 220–240 indicates the selling price of home between $220,000 and less than $240,000, and so on. The histogram is a plot of frequency distribution and is an excellent way of summarizing data sets. Figure 4.3 shows the percent for each category. Figure 4.4 shows a histogram with a normal curve superimposed. The graph shows that the home price data has a symmetrical shape, which is characterized by the normal distribution.

Graphical Summary of Data

This option provides useful statistics of the data along with graphs. The graphical summary of 300 home prices is shown in Figure 4.5.

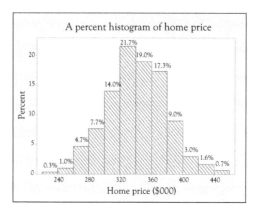

Figure 4.3 Percent histogram of home price

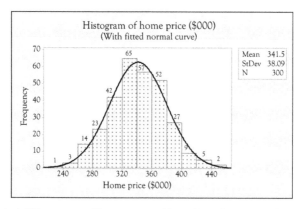

Figure 4.4 Histogram of home price ($000) with a normal curve

The summary report provides the plot of the data in form of a histogram with a normal curve superimposed. A box-plot of the data is shown below the histogram. Both of these plots—histogram and the box plot—summarize the data and provide information about the distribution of home price. On the right hand side, the calculated statistics are displayed. These statistics give us an idea about the average and the median house price along with the minimum, maximum, and the standard deviation. Several other statistics are calculated which are extremely useful in analyzing the data.

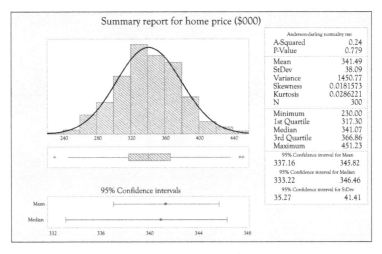

Figure 4.5 Summary report of home price ($000)

Graphical Display of Variation

Variation is one of the most important aspects of statistical analysis. Statistics is the science of variation and allows us to study variation. Almost all data show variation. The measurement and reduction of variation is one of the major objectives of quality programs. The following Figures 4.6 and 4.7 give us an idea about the variation in the data visually.

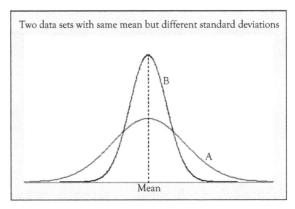

Figure 4.6 Data sets A and B with same mean but different variations

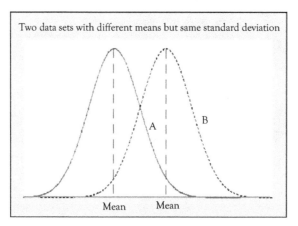

Figure 4.7 Data sets A and B with same variation but different means

Data Visualization: Conventional and Simple Techniques

In this section, we discuss the most widely used data visualization techniques. These graphical displays are most effective and useful in displaying the main features, drawing conclusions, and making decisions from the data.

Stem-and-Leaf Plot

Stem-and-Leaf plot is a very efficient way of displaying data and checking the variation and shape of the distribution. This plot is obtained by dividing each data value into two parts; stem and leaf. For example, if the data are two-digit numbers, e.g., 34, 56, 67, and so on, then the first number (the tens digit) is considered the stem value, and the second number (the ones digit) is considered the leaf value. Thus, in data value 56, 5 is the stem and 6 is the leaf. In a three-digit data value, the first two digits are considered the stem and the third digit as the leaf.

Example 4.2

The stem-and leaf plot in Figure 4.8 shows the number of orders received per day by a company. It is convenient to construct the plot using sorted

(1)	(2)	(3)
1	9	2
2	10	3
5	11	245
7	12	78
8	13	2
11	14	137
15	15	1229
22	16	2266778
27	17	01599
(11)	18	00013346799
17	19	03346
12	20	4679
8	21	0177
4	22	45
2	23	18

(a) How many days were studied? 55 (*obtained by adding the numbers above and below the row median row that is,* 27+11+17)

(b) How many observations are in the fourth class? 2

(c) What are the smallest and largest orders? 92, 238

(d) List the actual values in the sixth class? 141, 143, 147

(e) How many days did the firm receive less than 140 orders? 8

(f) How many days did the firm receive 200 or more orders? 12

(g) How many days did the firm receive 180 orders? 3

(h) What is the middle value? 180

(i) What can you say about the shape of the data? *Left or negatively skewed*

Figure 4.8 Stem-and-Leaf of orders received

data. There are three columns in the plot. The first column (labeled: 1) shows the cumulative count of the number of observations, the second (middle) column (labeled: 2) shows the stem values and the numbers following the second column (labeled: 3) represent the leaves. The first row has the following values:

1   9   2

This means that there is one observation in this row, the stem value is 9, and the leaf value is 2. Thus first value is 92. The second row also has one value in this row with a stem-value of 10 and the leaf value of 3.

2   10   3

The first column in the second row shows the cumulative count of observations up to this point. This value is 2. This means that there are two observations up to this row (1 in the first row and 1 value in the second row); the stem is 10 and the leaf value is 3, making the value in the second row 103.

Refer to Figure 4.8, column 1 again. The values from the top are 1, 2, 5, 7, 8, 11, 15, 22, and 27. This means that there are 27 observations up to row 9. The next number is 11, which is enclosed in a parenthesis: (11). This indicates that there are 11 observations in this row and this row contains the *median value* of the data. Once the median is determined, the count begins starting from the bottom row. Look into the bottom row that shows

2   23   18

This indicates there are two observations in this row, which are 231 and 238.

We can see from the earlier figure that the shape of the data is left skewed or negatively skewed, the minimum value is 92—the first value in the first row and the maximum value is 238, the last value. To find the total number of observations, add the observations in the median row, which is (11) and the observations above and below the median row; that is, 27+11+17=55. The stem-and-leaf can be used to obtain the information shown in the second column in Figure 4.8.

Box-Plots

The box-plot displays the smallest and the largest values in the data along with the three quartiles: Q_1, Q_2, and Q_3. The display of these five numbers (known as five measure summary) may be used to study the shape of the distribution and draw conclusion from the data. Different types of box plots can be created from the data. Some of these plots are shown as follows.

Example of Box Plots

The waiting times for 50 patients in an outpatient hospital clinic are shown in the following Table 4.4. The sorted values (the waiting time arranged in increasing order) are in Table 4.5.

The descriptive statistics showing the five measure summary of the data was calculated using MINITAB. The results are shown in Table 4.5.

From the previous table, the five measure summary calculated is:

Minimum value=6.8 minutes, Q1=10.48 minutes, Q2=11.80 minutes, Q3=13.10 minutes, and Maximum value=16.6 minutes.

The box plot displays these five measures. The box plot in Figure 4.9 shows that the minimum and maximum waiting times are 6.8 and 16.6 minutes. For 25 percent of the patients, the waiting time is less than 10.48 minutes, whereas 75 percent of the patients wait more than 10.48 minutes. The median waiting time is 11.8 minutes, which means that for 50 percent of the patients the waiting time is less than 11.8 minutes. While for the other 50 percent, the waiting time is more than 11.8 minutes.

Table 4.4 Waiting time data

Waiting time(min.)														
6.8	9.9	11.0	11.8	12.6	14.0	16.0	8.0	10.1	11.1	11.8	12.6	14.0	16.6	8.2
10.2	11.3	11.9	12.6	14.0	8.8	10.4	11.4	12.0	12.7	14.2	9.0	10.5	11.5	12.0
13.0	14.3	9.1	10.7	11.6	12.1	13.1	14.4	9.3	10.8	11.7	12.2	13.1	14.5	9.5
10.8	11.7	12.5	13.3	14.5										

Table 4.5 Descriptive statistics of waiting time

Descriptive statistics of waiting time									
Variable	N	N*	Mean	SE Mean	StDev	Minimum	Q1	Median	Q3
Waiting Time	50	0	11.784	0.289	2.045	6.800	10.475	11.800	13.100
Maximum									
16.600									

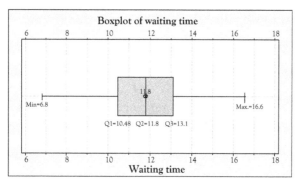

Figure 4.9 Box plot of waiting time data

The distribution of waiting time is approximately symmetrical. The median or Q2 line divides the box in approximately two halves. Also, the distance from the minimum time to Q1 is approximately equal to the distance between Q3 and maximum. The mean or average waiting time is 11.8 minutes. Which is equal to the median (Q2 value from the earlier table). Therefore, the distribution of the waiting time is symmetrical.

More Applications of Box Plot

This plot in Figure 4.10 is useful in monitoring one variable of interest (shaft diameter in this case) over several days or shifts. The box plots for each day of production are plotted. These plots are useful in monitoring the variation and shift in the process over time.

Figure 4.11 shows the box plots of five samples each of size 36 from a shaft manufacturing process. Four machines were used in the production

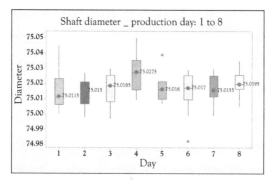

Figure 4.10 Box plots of shaft diameter over a period of 8 days

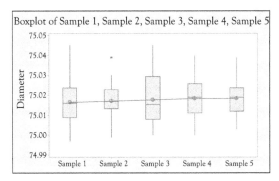

Figure 4.11 Box-plots for 5 samples of same product

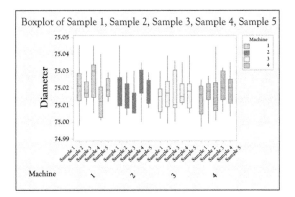

Figure 4.12 Box plots of samples vs. machines

of these shafts. The plot can be used to check the consistency and distribution of the diameters with respect to the machines.

Figure 4.12 shows the variation of the box plots where samples from each of the four machines in production are plotted separately. These plots can be used to check the consistency and distribution of the diameter with respect to each machine. Suppose you want to check the consistency of the diameters of five samples with respect to three machine operators. The plots in Figure 4.13 can be used for this purpose.

Dot Plots

A *dot plot* may be used to study the shape of the distribution or to compare two or more than two sets of data. In a dot plot, the horizontal axis

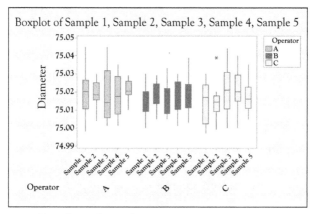

Figure 4.13 Box plots of samples vs. operators

shows the range of values in the data. Each observation is represented by a dot placed above the axis. If the data value repeat, the dots are piled up at that location, showing a dot for each repeated value.

Example 4.3

Figure 4.14 shows the dot plot of the data that represents the spot speed 100 cars at 65 mph speed limit zone. The dot plot in Figure 4.15 shows the number of cars sold by a dealership over a period of 100 days. The numbers of cars are the total number sold at four different locations of the same dealership. The horizontal axis shows the number of cars sold

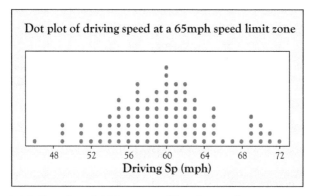

Figure 4.14 Dot plot of 100 cars at 65 mph speed zone

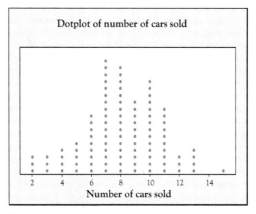

Figure 4.15 Dot plot of number of cars sold

and the vertical axis shows the days. The first value on the horizontal axis is 2 with three dots above it. This means that three cars were sold in the first two days. The total number of dots is 100 indicating the number sold over 100 days.

Bar Charts

Bar charts are one of the widely used charts to display categorical data. These charts can be used to display monthly or quarterly sales, revenue, and profits for a company. Figure 4.16 shows the monthly sales of a company. Figure 4.17 shows a variation of the bar chart.

Figure 4.16 A bar chart of monthly sales

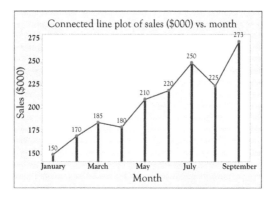

Figure 4.17 Connected line over the bar chart of sales vs. month

Example 4.4 More Examples of Bar Chart Categorical Data

(a) *A Vertical Bar Chart.* Figure 4.18 shows a vertical bar chart showing the gold price from 1975 to 2011.

The previous chart is useful in visualizing the trend and also the percent increase and decrease in the value over the years. For example: Percent increase in the price of gold (per ounce) between 1980 and 2011 can be determined as:

The price in 1980=$594.90 per ounce and the price in 2011=$1680.0.

Therefore, the percent increase=(1680–594.90)/594.90*100=182.4%.

(b) *A Cluster Bar Chart:* A cluster bar chart can be used to compare data categories. An example of cluster bar chart showing zone wise

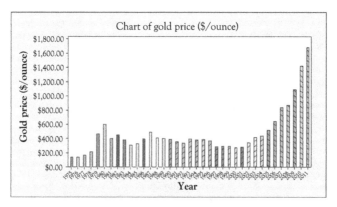

Figure 4.18 A vertical bar chart of gold price

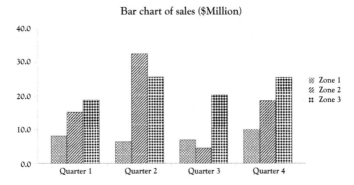

Figure 4.19 A cluster bar chart showing zone wise sales

quarterly sales of a company is shown in Figure 4.19. In this plot the three zones are clusters for each quarter.

Another Example of Cluster Bar Chart

Another example of a cluster bar chart would be to compare the quarterly sales for the past four years in which the cluster is the group of the four quarters of each year. Figure 4.20 shows another cluster bar chart.

(c) *Stacked Bar Chart*

Stacked bar charts are also used to compare different measure of data categories. In the most common form, a stacked bar chart displays a count of a category. These charts can also be created to

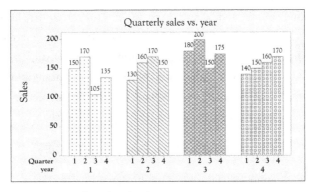

Figure 4.20 Quarterly sales for four years

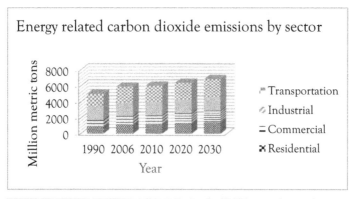

	1990	2006	2010	2020	2030
Residential	961.7	1,203.8	1,258.6	1,323.7	1,450.8
Commercial	787.6	1,045.8	1,079.2	1,265.3	1,474.1
Industrial	1,679.7	1,651.8	1,692.7	1,718.1	1,732.8
Transportation	1,582.6	1,989.0	1,980.1	2,077.0	2,193.3

Figure 4.21 A stacked bar chart of carbon dioxide emissions by sector

represent a function of a category (such as the mean, or sum) or the summary values. Figure 4.21 shows a stacked bar chart. This chart shows carbon dioxide emissions by different sectors—residential, commercial, industrial, and transportation. Each of these sectors is categorized by year and is displayed as a stacked chart.

Describing, Summarizing, and Graphing Categorical Variables

Categorical data are the data arranged in classes or categories; whereas continuous data are numerical measurements of quantities such as length, height, time, volume, temperature, and so on. Categorical data also result from the classification of elements into groups based on some common attribute. For example, we can group the companies into "small," "medium," or "large," based on the number of employees. We can also group people based on their annual income and their occupation. In this section, we will provide examples of bar charts describing categorical variables.

Example 4.5 Creating a Bar Chart from a Simple Tally

A tally is a count or percentage of number of cases in a category. Table 4.6 contains partial data of the ratings for Product 1 for a sample

Table 4.6 Rating for Product 1 provided by 200 customers using a scale of 0 to 5

Product 1 Rating																							
0	1	3	3	4	5	1	4	3	3	4	5	1	0	3	4	5	3	4	3	5	0	1
3	4	5	4	3	2	1	4	3	0	0	0	3	3	1	1	1	1	4	4	4	5	4
5	5	3	2	3	3	4	4	4	4	4	5	3	2	4	5	3	1	4	5	5	0	0
2	3	5	4	0	0	0	3	4	3	2	4	4	4	4	4	5	3	3	0	4	4	3
:																						
3	5	4	4	5	3	3	2	2	5	4	3	2	1	1	2	3	4	5	4	3	2	1

of 200 product users. The variable product rating is a categorical variable with a scale ranging from 0 to 5 (0=Unacceptable, 1=Fair, 2=Poor, 3=Satisfactory, 4=Good, 5=Excellent). [Table 4.7 provides the ratings for Product 2]. It shows partial data. Unlike Table 4.6, the data is not coded for Product 2.

The data in Tables 4.6 and 4.7 convey very little meaning. To make the ratings data more meaningful, we prepare a simple tally for Product 1 and 2 and present the information in a graphical form using bar charts. The tables and graphs of the product ratings will immediately tell us how these products were rated by the customers.

Before we plot the ratings data, we create a tally shown in Table 4.8 followed by bar charts.

Table 4.7 Rating for Product 2 provided by 200 customers (not coded)

Product 2 rating (partial data)					
Satisfactory	Good	Very good	Excellent	Poor	Fair
Satisfactory	Good	Satisfactory	Good	Very good	Excellent
Poor	Satisfactory	Good	Very good	Good	Very good
:					
Very good	Excellent	Poor	Fair	Satisfactory	Good

Table 4.8 Tally for Product 1 rating

Tally for discrete variables: Product 1 rating				
1 Rating	Count	Percent	CumCnt	CumPct
0	20	10.00	20	10.00
1	23	11.50	43	21.50
2	21	10.50	64	32.00
3	45	22.50	109	54.50
4	59	29.50	168	84.00
5	32	16.00	200	100.00
N=	200			

Tallies and Graphical Displays of Product 1 Rating

Figures 4.22(a) and (b) show the bar charts of Product 1 rating. The figure on the left clearly shows that 59 of the 200 users rated the product as "good." This is equivalent to 29.5 percent shown on the right figure. These visual displays are very useful in the decision making process.

Tallies and Graphical Displays of Product 2 Rating

The tally and bar chart for Product 2 ratings are shown in Table 4.9 and Figures 4.23(a) and (b). Note that the ratings were not coded for this product.

Table 4.9 Tally for Product 2 rating

Tally for discrete variables: Product 2 rating				
Rating	Count	Percent	CumCnt	CumPct
Excellent	30	13.64	30	13.64
Fair	18	8.18	48	21.82
Good	57	25.91	105	47.73
Poor	25	11.36	130	59.09
Satisfactory	49	22.27	179	81.36
Very good	41	18.64	220	100.00
N=	220			

Table 4.10 Cross-table employment status, degree major and gender

Tabulated statistics: Employment status, Major, Gender

Results for Gender = Female

Rows: Employment Status   Columns: Major

	1	2	3	4	5	All
Employed	5	7	26	26	16	80
Self-employed	1	4	8	6	3	22
All	6	11	34	32	19	102

Cell Contents: Count

Results for Gender = Male

Rows: Employment Status   Columns: Major

	1	2	3	4	5	All
Employed	9	22	9	20	15	75
Self-employed	3	6	2	11	1	23
All	12	28	11	31	16	98

Cell Contents: Count

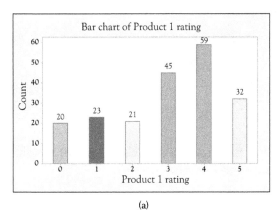

(a)

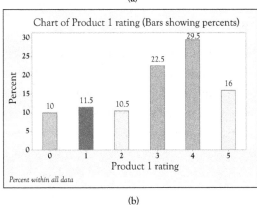

(b)

Figure 4.22 (a) Bar chart of Product 1 rating. (b) Bar chart of Product 1 rating (bars showing percent)

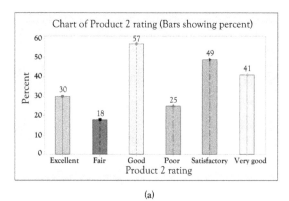

(a)

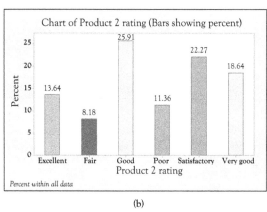

(b)

Figure 4.23 (a) Bar chart of Product 2 rating. (b) Bar chart of Product 2 rating (bars showing percent)

Example 4.6 Cross Tabulation with Two and Three Categorical Variables

The data for variables: Gender (male, female); degree major (1=computer science, 2=engineering, 3=social science, 4=business, 5=other); and employment status (employed, self-employed) are summarized in Table 4.10. Using cross tabulation, we construct bar charts to show the employment status and degree major for the male and female respondents. The bar charts from the table are shown in Figures 4.24 and 4.25. The figures are self-explanatory. These visual displays clearly summarize the data and reveal important features that are not apparent from the raw data or the tables created.

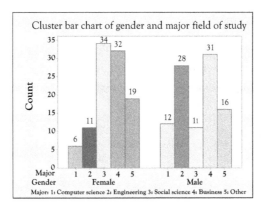

Figure 4.24 A bar chart of gender and Major

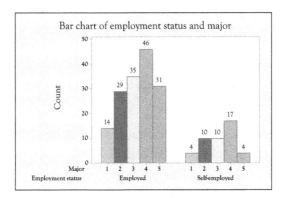

Figure 4.25 A bar chart of employment status and major

Pie Charts

A pie chart is used to show the relative magnitudes of parts to a whole. In this chart relative frequencies of each group of data are plotted. A circle is constructed and is divided into distinct sections. Each section represents one group of data. The area of each section is determined by multiplying the relative frequency of each section by the angle of a circle. Since there are 360° in a circle, the relative frequency of each section is multiplied by 360° to obtain the correct number of degrees for each section. Some examples of pie charts and their variations are shown in the following pages.

Example 4.7 A Simple Pie Chart

Figure 4.26 shows a simple pie chart of U.S. Federal budget expenditures. The chart clearly shows the major categories along with the dollar values and the percentages. Several variations of this chart can be created.

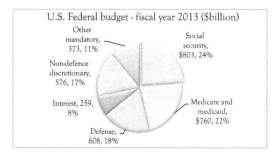

Figure 4.26 U.S. Federal budget

Example 4.8 Variations of Pie Chart: Bar of a Pie Chart

Figure 4.27 shows a variation of the pie chart. This chart is commonly known as *Bar of Pie*. A bar chart is created that is an extension of the pie chart. The purpose of the bar chart is to show the important features of one of the main categories. The pie chart shows the energy consumption for 2014 by different energy sources. The renewable energy usage is 10 percent of the total and this category comprises of different categories, the percentages of which are shown using a bar chart.

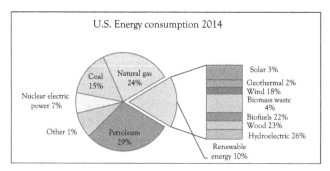

Figure 4.27 Bar of Pie chart

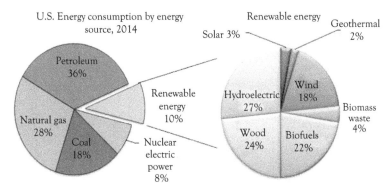

Figure 4.28 Pie of Pie chart

Example 4.9 Another Variation of Pie Chart: Pie of a Pie Chart

Figure 4.28 Displays a *Pie of Pie* chart. In this chart, the bar is replaced with a pie chart to show the proportions of a category of interest.

Interval Plots

The interval plot displays means and/or confidence intervals for one or more variables. This plot is useful for assessing the measure of central tendency and variability of data. The default confidence interval is 95 percent; however, this can be changed. We will demonstrate the interval plot using the production data of beverage cans. This data contains the amount of beverage in 16 oz. cans from five different production lines. The operations manager suspects that the mean content of the cans differs from line to line. He randomly selected five cans from each line and measured the contents. The interval plot from five different production lines is shown in Figure 4.29.

Example 4.10 Interval Plot Showing the Variation in Sample Data

Interval plot is also useful in visualizing the variation in samples. The data plotted shows 20 samples each of size 10 of finished inside diameter of piston ring (in mm). We want to investigate sample to sample variation and the mean for each sample by constructing an interval plot. Figure 4.30 shows the plot.

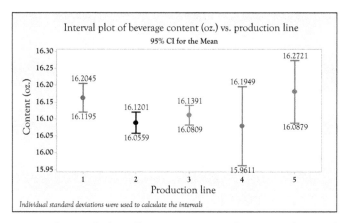

Figure 4.29 Interval plot of beverage content from 5 production lines

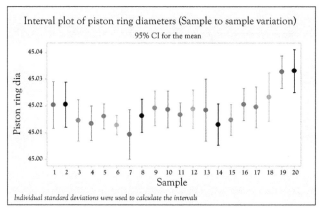

Figure 4.30 Interval plot of piston ring diameter

Time Series Plots

A time series plots the data over time. The graph plots the (x_i, y_i) pairs of points and connects these plots using straight lines where the x values are time. The plot is helpful in visualizing a trend or pattern in a data set. In Figure 4.31, a time series plot of demand data over time is explained. Figure 4.32 shows the sales over time for a company. The data plotted shows weekly demand data for the past 60 weeks. Each quarter is divided into 13 weeks.

Figure 4.33 shows the sales and short term forecast over a period of 60 weeks. The forecast is plotted using a dotted line. Notice how the

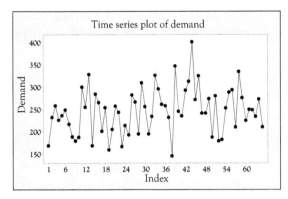

Figure 4.31 A simple time series plot of demand

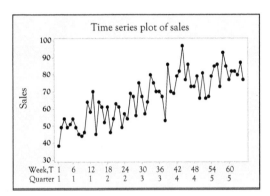

Figure 4.32 A simple time series plot of sales Data

Figure 4.33 A multiple time series plot showing sales and forecast

forecast follows the trend in the sales. Figure 4.34 shows a seasonal pattern for the furnace filter demand and Figure 4.35 shows an increasing trend in sales over time.

In all of the aforementioned time series plots, the trends and patterns cannot be seen unless the data are plotted.

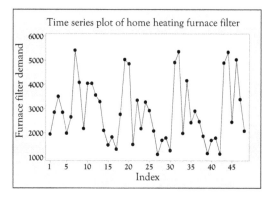

Figure 4.34 A time series plot showing a seasonal pattern

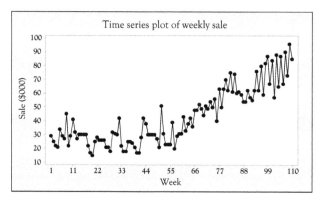

Figure 4.35 A time series plot showing a trend

Sequence Plot: Plot of Process Data

A sequence plot is used to show the evolution of a measured characteristic over time. This plot is similar to a time-series plot, with the time plotted on the horizontal axis and the corresponding process characteristic on the vertical axis. The sequence plot is a simple plot showing the behavior of the process over time. The variation or the trend in the process can be seen easily from this plot. The plot can also be used to see the deviation of a process from a specified target value.

Example 4.11

The data in Table 4.11 list the deviation (in 0.00025-inch units) of the diameter of 90 machined shafts from the target value. In these data, 0 means that the measured diameter was right on target, 2 means that the measured diameter was 0.0005 inch above the target value; whereas, a 3 means that the measured diameter was 0.00075 above the target value. We constructed a sequence plot of the data and interpreted the results.

Figures 4.36 and 4.37 show two variations of the sequence plot. Figure 4.36 shows large deviation for part numbers 27, 30, 44, 45, and 72. The rest of the measurements do not show large deviation. To see if all the measurements are within the specified limits, we can also plot the specification limits on the plot (see Figure 4.37).

Suppose that the specification limits on the shaft diameter are 2±0.0025 inch. This means that in Figure 4.37 the target value coded 0 is 2, the upper limit is 10 (which is 0.00025*10=0.0025), and the lower limit is –10. Figure 4.37 shows the sequence plot with specification limits. From this plot, you can see that part numbers 27, 44, and 72 are outside of the specification limits. At this stage, identifying the problems and taking corrective actions will bring the products under control.

Table 4.11 Measured diameter of a machined part

Diameter deviation from target [Coded in 0.00025 inch deviation from target]												
–4	–1	1	–5	6	–1	6	0	2	–2	–2	4	–5
0	–4	1	–4	0	–3	–4	–5	–3	2	0	–3	2
17	1	6	–8	2	1	2	–1	4	–1	2	–4	2
0	3	1	2	12	–8	2	2	1	2	1	2	7
–1	–5	–1	–1	0	1	1	–1	9	–1	0	–3	–4
3	–1	3	–2	–2	0	–12	2	0	2	0	–1	–2
–5	–2	–2	2	0	2	4	6	–3	0	7	–6	

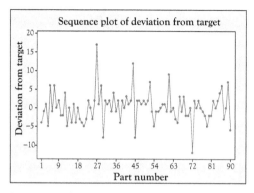

Figure 4.36 Sequence plot of the measurements on machined parts

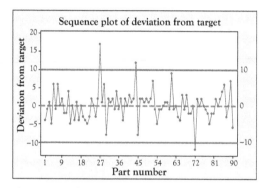

Figure 4.37 Sequence plot with specification limits

Example 4.12 Sequence Plot

Because of increased competition, a large pizza chain is going to launch a new marketing campaign. The chain would like to advertise that they will make the delivery in 15 minutes or less; otherwise, the pizza is free. Before they launch the campaign, the pizza chain would like to study the current delivery process. If the current process indicates large variations in the delivery time, the causes of variation will be studied and corrective actions will be taken to meet the target delivery time of 15 minutes or less. The data for the delivery time (in minutes) of 120 deliveries by different carriers were collected. A sequence plot of the delivery time data is shown in Figure 4.38. We would like to analyze the graph to get an idea of the variation in the current delivery process. The plot will also tell us whether the current process is meeting the target time of 15 minutes or less.

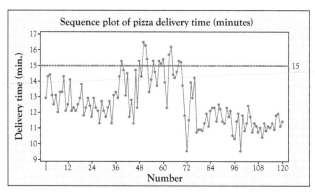

Figure 4.38 Sequence plot of pizza delivery time

From Figure 4.38, we see that the delivery times vary considerably. In some places, the process shows little variation. In others, it varies significantly. A line is drawn at 15 minutes to show the target value. The values above this line indicate delivery exceeding 15 minutes. There are 13 or 10.8 percent (13/120=0.108*100) or approximately 11 percent deliveries exceeding 15 minutes. This amounts to 108,000 missed deliveries in a million deliveries. The pizza chain needs to study the causes of variation to stabilize this process and meet the target delivery.

Connected Line Plot

This plot connects each of the data values using a line. The graph is very useful in visualizing the trend in the data. Figure 4.39 is an example of connected line plot. The plot clearly shows the trend in the gold price over the years.

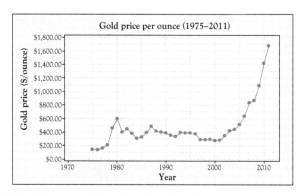

Figure 4.39 Connected line plot of gold price per ounce

Area Graph

The area graph is used to examine trends in multiple time series as well as each series' contribution to the sum. The area graph in Figure 4.40 shows the monthly production of crude oil (in thousands of barrels) from 1920 to 2014.

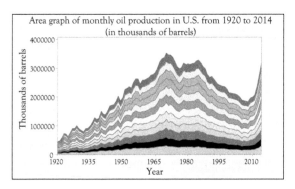

Figure 4.40 Area graph of monthly oil production in U.S.

Note: The area below each line represents the cumulative total.

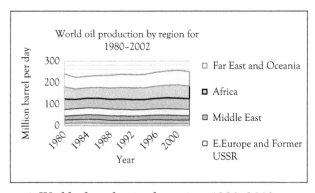

Figure 4.41 World oil production by region, 1980–2002

Example 4.13 Another Example of Area Graph: World Oil Production

The area graph of world oil production (in millions of barrels) from 1980 to 2002 is shown in Figure 4.41. Note that the area below each line represents the cumulative total.

	1980	1982	1984	1986	1988	1990	1992	1994	1996	1998	2000	2002
North America	11.7	12.5	13.1	12.3	10.2	10	10	10	10	10	10	10
Cent. & South America	15	15.9	16.8	16.6	15.2	15.2	15.5	16.2	17.4	17.2	16.4	16.2
Europe	18	19.3	20.7	20.7	20.5	20.5	19.5	19.8	21.7	21.9	21	20
E.Europe & Former USSR	30	30.8	31.5	31.7	31	30	28.6	28.1	28.9	29.6	30	30
Middle East	48.8	43.7	45.1	46	46.3	47.7	48	47.7	48.7	50.6	50.8	49.1
Africa	56	48.2	48.2	50.1	51.5	53.4	53.9	53.4	56.1	58	60.1	58
Far East & Oceania	59.5	52.6	52.9	54.4	58.1	60.6	60.4	60.8	64.4	65.4	67.3	66.6

Source: Energy information administration

Measures of Association Between Two Quantitative Variables: The Scatter Plot and the Coefficient of Correlation

Describing the relationship between two quantitative variables is called a *bivariate relationship*. One way of investigating this relationship is to construct a *scatter plot*. A scatter plot is a two-dimensional plot where one variable is plotted along the vertical axis and the other along the horizontal axis. The pairs of points (x_i, y_i) plotted on the scatter plot are helpful in *visually* examining the relationship between the two variables.

In a scatter plot, one of the variables is considered a *dependent variable* and the other an *independent variable*. The data value is thought of as having a (x, y) pair. Thus, we have (x_i, y_i), $i = 1, 2, \ldots, n$ pairs. Computer packages, such as EXCEL and MINITAB provide several options for constructing scatter plots.

Example 4.14

Figure 4.42 shows a scatter plot depicting the relationship between sales and advertising expenditure for a company.

From Figure 4.42 we can see a distinct increase in sales associated with the higher values of advertisement dollars. This is an indication of a *positive relationship* between the two variables. This means that an increase in one variable leads to an increase in the other one.

Example 4.15

Figure 4.43 shows the relationship between the home heating cost and the average outside temperature. This plot shows a tendency for the points to follow a straight line with a negative slope. This means that

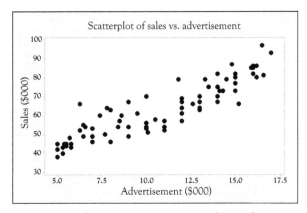

Figure 4.42 Scatter plot showing a positive relationship

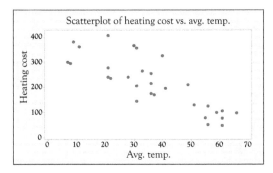

Figure 4.43 A scatter plot depicting inverse relationship between heating cost and temperature

there is an *inverse or negative relationship* between the heating cost and the average temperature. As the average outside temperature increases, the home heating cost goes down. Figure 4.44 shows a weak or no relationship between quality rating and material cost of a product.

Example 4.16

In Figure 4.45, we have plotted the summer temperature and the amount of electricity used (in millions of kilowatts). The plotted points in this figure can be well approximated by a straight line. Therefore, we can conclude that a linear relationship exists between the two variables.

The linear relationship can be explained by fitting a regression line over the scatter plot as shown in Figure 4.46. The equation of this line is

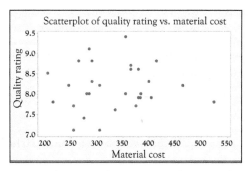

Figure 4.44 *Scatter plot of quality rating and material cost (weak/no relationship)*

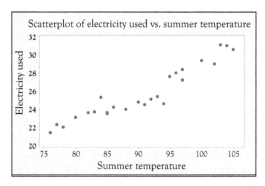

Figure 4.45 *A scatter plot of summer temperature and electricity used*

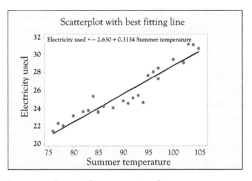

Figure 4.46 *Scatter plot with regression line*

used to describe the relationship between the two variables—temperature and electricity used.

The regression line shown in Figure 4.46 is known as the line of "best fit." This is the best fitting line through the data points and is uniquely determined using a mathematical technique known as the *least squares method.*

Example 4.17 Scatter Plot Showing a Non-linear Relationship Between x and y

In many cases, the relationship between the two variables under study may be non-linear. Figure 4.47 shows the plot of the yield of a chemical process at different temperatures.

The scatter plot of the variables temperature (x) and the yield (y) shows a non-linear relationship that can be best approximated by a quadratic equation. The equation of the fitted curve in Figure 4.47 obtained using a computer package is $y = -1022 + 320.3x - 1.054x^2$. This equation can be used to predict the yield (y) for a particular temperature (x).

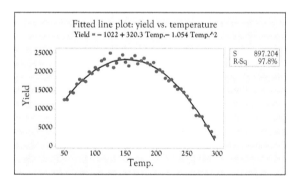

Figure 4.47 Scatter plot with best fitting curve

The Coefficient of Correlation

The sample coefficient of correlation (r_{xy}) is a measure of relative strength of a linear relationship between two quantitative variables. This is a unitless quantity. The coefficient of correlation has a value between -1 and $+1$ where a value of -1 indicates a perfect negative correlation and a value of $+1$ indicates a perfect positive correlation.

If the scatter plot shows a positive linear relationship between x and y, the calculated coefficient of correlation will be positive; whereas, a negative relationship between x and y on the scatter plot will provide a negative value of the coefficient of correlation.

Note that a value of correlation coefficient r_{xy} closer to +1, indicates a strong positive relationship between x and y; whereas, a value of r_{xy} closer to –1 indicates a strong negative correlation between the two variables x and y. A value of r_{xy} that is zero or close to zero, indicates no or weak correlation between x and y.

Examples of Coefficient of Correlation

Figures 4.48(a) through (d) show several scatter plots with the correlation coefficient.

Figure 4.48(a) shows a positive correlation between the sales and profit with a correlation coefficient value r = +0.979. Figure 4.48(b) shows a positive relationship between the sales and advertisement expenditures with a calculated correlation coefficient r = +0.902. Figure 4.48(c) shows a negative relationship between the heating cost and the average temperature. Therefore, the coefficient of correlation (r) for this plot is negative r = –0.827. The correlation for the scatter plot in Figure 4.48(d) indicates a weak relationship between the quality rating and the material cost. This

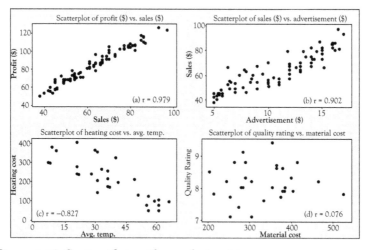

Figure 4.48 Scatter plots with correlation (r)

can also be seen from the coefficient of correlation which shows a value of $r = 0.076$. These graphs are very helpful in describing bivariate relationships or the relationship between the two quantitative variables and can be easily created using computer packages such as, MINITAB or EXCEL.

Note that the plots in Figure 4.48(a) and (b) shows strong positive correlation; (c) shows a negative correlation while (d) shows a weak correlation.

Scatter Plot with Regression

A fitted line over the scatter plot provides the best fitting line through the data points. The equation of this line can be determined which is known as the regression equation. The equation can be used to predict the

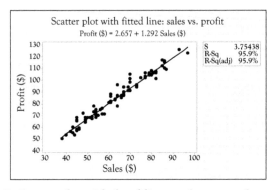

Figure 4.49 Scatter plot with fitted line—sales vs. profit

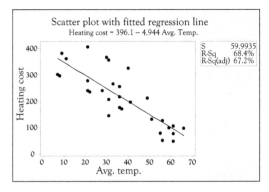

Figure 4.50 Scatter plot with fitted line—heating cost vs. average temperature

dependent variable (the *y* variable) using the independent variable or the *x* variable. These plots are shown in Figures 4.49 and 4.50.

Exploring the Relationship
Between Three Variables: Bubble Plot

The bubble plot is used to explore the relationships among three variables on a single plot. The plot uses bubbles to plot the third variable hence the name *bubble plot*. Similar to a scatter plot that is used to explore the relationship between two variables, the bubble plot uses bubbles of different sizes to represent the third variable. The area of the bubble represents the value of the third variable.

Example 4.18

The bubble plots in Figures 4.51 and 4.52 investigate the relationship between three variables—the advertisement expenditure, sales (both in thousands of dollars) and store size for a large retailer. The retailer has different sizes of store that can be classified as small, medium, and large.

In Figures 4.51, the small, medium, and large store sizes are labeled 1, 2, and 3 respectively; whereas in Figure 4.52, the store sizes are labeled not numbered. The bubble graphs show that an increase in advertisement expenditure leads to increased sales but the large stores not necessarily have the largest sales.

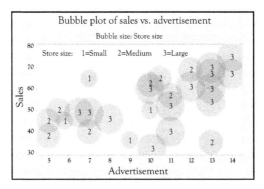

Figure 4.51 Bubble plot showing the relationship between sales, advertisement, and store size

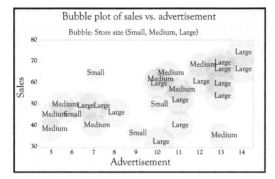

Figure 4.52 Bubble plot showing the relationship between sales, advertisement, and store size—store size not coded

Example 4.19 Additional Examples of Bubble Plots

The bubble plots in Figures 4.53 through 4.54 show some more variations.

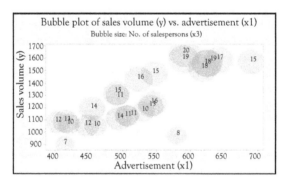

Figure 4.53 Bubble plot showing the relationship between sales, advertisement, and number of sales person

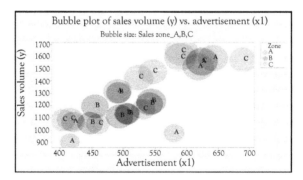

Figure 4.54 Bubble plot showing the relationship between sales, advertisement, and sales zones

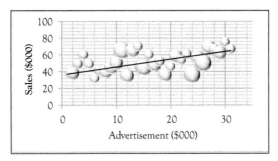

Figure 4.54(a) Bubble plot showing the relationship between sales and advertisement with a trend line

Some other useful visual tools: Matrix plots, 3-D plots

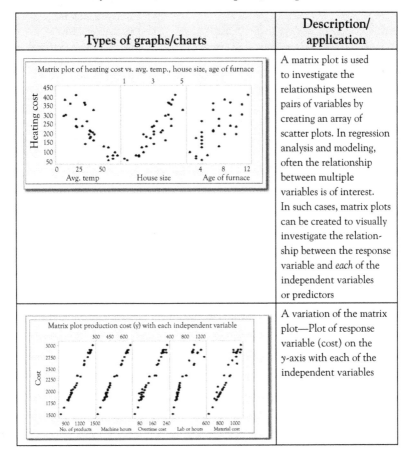

Types of graphs/charts	Description/ application
Matrix plot of heating cost vs. avg. temp., house size, age of furnace	A matrix plot is used to investigate the relationships between pairs of variables by creating an array of scatter plots. In regression analysis and modeling, often the relationship between multiple variables is of interest. In such cases, matrix plots can be created to visually investigate the relationship between the response variable and *each* of the independent variables or predictors
Matrix plot production cost (y) with each independent variable	A variation of the matrix plot—Plot of response variable (cost) on the y-axis with each of the independent variables

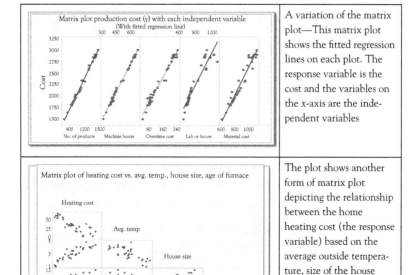

Matrix plot production cost (y) with each independent variable (With fitted regression line)	A variation of the matrix plot—This matrix plot shows the fitted regression lines on each plot. The response variable is the cost and the variables on the x-axis are the independent variables
Matrix plot of heating cost vs. avg. temp., house size, age of furnace	The plot shows another form of matrix plot depicting the relationship between the home heating cost (the response variable) based on the average outside temperature, size of the house (×1,000 square feet), and the life of the furnace (years) by creating an array of scatter plots

The next chapter deals with exploring large databases and advanced techniques of data visualization, data dashboards, and their applications.

CHAPTER 5

Data Visualization with Big Data

Chapter Highlights

Data Visualization and Visual Analytics

Introduction and Applications of Big Data

Software and Applications of Big Data in Different Areas

Government Manufacturing/Operations Health Care Education Businesses Media Internet of Things (IoT) Real Estate Science and research

Fundamental Concepts in Data Visualization

Different Forms of Data Visualization

Information Visualization or Information graphics or infographics

Characteristics of Effective Graphical Displays

Quantitative Messages Conveyed by Simple Data Visualization

Software Tools for Data Visualization

Terminology for Data Visualization

Types of Information Displays

Two Primary Types of Information Displays

Data Visualization and Information Visualization

Data Visualization Software Applications

Summary

Data Visualization and Visual Analytics

Data visualization is a form of visual communication that presents the data in graphical form. It involves creating charts, graphs, and other visual tools that also include flowcharts to communicate the information in the data effectively. The previous chapters in this book presented numerous graphical displays created from both variables and attributes data that are powerful visualization tools. One of the major objectives of data visualization is to reveal the essential characteristics of data that may not be apparent otherwise. Data visualization makes complex and large data understandable. *Visual analytics* is an added feature in data visualization. Several data visualization software programs are equipped with interactive visualization that aids in the processing and analysis of data by drilling down into the graphical displays. A number of charts and graphs can be created from the same data set that helps to visualize different features of the data and at the same time can answer *what if* questions. Visual analytics can also be used interactively with continuously changing data to identify new patterns. In this age of *big data*, data visualization and visual analytics are becoming a critical part of data analysis. Data in their raw form including those in the databases of companies are not very useful unless processed and analyzed. Presenting data visually using charts and graphs shows the patterns and relationships of several variables simultaneously. At present, visualization with big data is becoming a requirement because of the increase in the volume of data being collected and stored. The term *data analytics* is often used with big data. It is the science of analyzing vast amount of data to draw meaningful conclusions and make better business decisions. In the field of science, data analytics helps to examine data to prove or disprove already known theories or models. The field of data analytics differs from *data mining* that examines vast amount of data using specially designed software and algorithms to identify patterns and relationships. Big data presents numerous challenges in storing, analyzing, processing, and communicating the huge amount of data. In this chapter we provide an overview of data visualization techniques using big data.

Introduction and Applications of Big Data

Big data refers to data set that is massive and ranges from terabytes to many petabytes. The processing and analysis of such data are beyond the capability of traditional software. Recently, specialized software and computer applications have been designed to store, analyze, visualize, and share large amounts of data. Big data is different from the conventional data in many aspects. Often, a "3Vs" model is used to distinguish big data from the conventional data. The 3Vs refer to volume, variety, and velocity. According to Gartner (2012): "Big data is high volume, high velocity, and/or high variety of data that require new forms of processing to enable enhanced decision making, insight discovery and process optimization." It is important to note that big data does not use sampling as in statistical analysis; it looks into the entire data set to visualize and observes what happens.

The big data may be available in real time that may continuously change (velocity). These data are drawn from text, images, audio, videos, and so on (variety). It is important to note that, besides descriptive statistics, the applications of big data involve inductive statistics that use inferential statistics and predictive modeling tools to make predictions of future behavior of the variables.

According to Martin big data possess the following characteristics:

[*"Big Data for Development: A Review of Promises and Challenges. Development Policy Review." martinhilbert.net. Retrieved* 2015-10-07]

Volume

It refers to the quantity of generated and stored data. The size of the data determines the value and potential insight and whether it can actually be considered big data or not.

Variety

This is the type and nature of the data. This helps people who analyze it to effectively use the resulting insight.

Velocity

It is the speed at which the data is generated and processed to meet the demands and challenges that lie in the path of growth and development.

Variability

Inconsistency of the data set can hamper the performance of processes and make it difficult to handle and manage.

Veracity

The quality of captured data can vary greatly, affecting accurate analysis.

Software and Applications of Big Data in Different Areas

Data visualization when combined with visual analytics allows creating different scenarios of the data and provides the user with the ability to experiment and extract useful information quickly. The techniques of visualization can help identify the problem areas, provide opportunities for improvement, identify the areas that need attention, and predict the future outcomes.

Due to the increasing need for storing, processing, and analyzing big data, there has been a significant increase in the software applications in this area. Software firms including *Software AG, Oracle Corporation, IBM, Microsoft, SAP, EMC, HP, Dell, Tableau Software, Dundas BI, Google*, and others have spent more than $15 billion on software firms specializing in data management and analytics. In 2010, this industry was worth more than $100 billion and was growing at almost 10 percent a year: about twice as fast as the software business as a whole [32].

Advancements in data visualization, visual analytics, business analytics, and big data analysis are helping to detect the areas where improvement efforts can be directed. They are also helping to improve decision making in critical areas, such as health care, employment, economic outlook and development/productivity, crime, security, education, natural disaster, and resource management [33][34][35] to name a few. However, they come with a number of challenges. These include inadequate technological infrastructure, privacy, appropriate methodology, and data preparation and management [33].

The following are some of the areas where big data and data visualization have been used successfully.

Government

United Sates of America: the Big Data Research and Development Initiative was announced by the Obama administration in 2012. The purpose was to explore how big data could be used to address the problems faced by the government. The research initiative in this area is evident from the fact that the U.S. government owns six of the 10 most powerful computers in the world. The U.S. National Security Agency (NSA) has initiated a project in Utah named *Utah Data Center*. This project will be able to handle large amount of information collected by NSA over the Internet. The center is expected to store a few *exabytes* [36][37][38] of data.

Manufacturing/Operations

In certain types of manufacturing environments including pharmaceuticals, mining, and chemicals, vast amount of data are needed to diagnose and correct process flaws. Because of the processing complexity involved in these processes and the number of factors involved, advanced analytics tools are being used to diagnose and correct the problems even in real time. Advanced analytics is the application of statistical and mathematical tools in detecting, analyzing, and improving the processes. These tools help managers and analysts to examine the historical data to identify the patterns and define relationships between the inputs and outputs of the process. This helps in determining the factors that have greatest influence on the process output and optimizing them. Neural-network techniques (a tool used in advanced analytics based on the way the human brain processes information) have also been used to measure and compare the relative impact of different process inputs on the output or yield.

The manufacturers have now access to real-time process data so that they can aggregate and perform advanced analytics to learn and optimize the processes. In biopharmaceuticals involving production of vaccines, hormones, and blood components that employ live, genetically engineered cells, there are hundreds of variables that need monitoring to ensure the purity. In these processes the variation of yield may be between 50 and 100 percent from batch to batch [http://mckinsey.com/how-big-data-can-improve-manufacturing]. These examples show the complexity of the processes that require vast amount of data to be analyzed to monitor and correct them. Applications of advanced analytics tools can help reduce process flow and optimize these processes.

Health Care

Big data in health care is improving public health. Some areas of applications include automated external and internal reporting of patient data, standardized medical terms and patient registries, improving profits, and reducing waste. Other applications in health care where big data is being helpful are: predicting epidemics, curing disease, improving the quality of life, and disease prevention. One of the major applications of big data in health care is in decoding entire DNA strings in minutes. This is helping to find new cures and to better understand and predict disease patterns.

Education

A *McKinsey Global Institute* study found a shortage of 1.5 million highly trained data professionals and managers [39] and a number of universities [40] have created masters programs to meet this demand.

Businesses

Businesses are using big data to understand and target customers, find areas of opportunities to improve businesses, and optimize business processes using predictive analytics. Big retailers like Walmart and Target are using big data to predict customer behaviors and to determine what products will sell. Big data analytics is helping in making appropriate and timely business decisions and is being applied in designing, managing, improving, and optimizing the supply chain. The radio frequency identification sensors and geographic positioning are used to track and optimize the delivery routes. Big data is also finding applications in improving the human resources (HR).

Media

Big data is now being used in media to target specific groups of customers to convey a message or content that is in line with the consumer's interest. Data mining tools play a vital role in capturing data and targeting consumers.

Internet of Things (IoT)

The Internet of things [*Main article: Internet of Things*] is a growing network of everyday objects from industrial machines to consumer goods that can share information and complete tasks. Soon, our cars, our homes, our major appliances, and even our city streets will be connected to the Internet—creating this network of objects that is called the Internet of things, or IoT in short. Made up of millions of sensors and devices that generate incessant streams of data, the IoT can be used to improve our lives and our businesses in many ways.

Business Applications:

- eBay.com uses two data warehouses at 7.5 *petabytes* (PB) and 40 PB as well as a 40 PB *Hadoop* cluster for search, consumer recommendations, and merchandising [41].
- Amazon.com handles millions of back-end operations every day, as well as queries from more than half a million third-party sellers. The core technology that keeps Amazon running is Linux-based and as of 2005 it had the world's three largest Linux databases, with capacities of 7.8 terabytes (TB), 18.5 TB, and 24.7 TB [42].
- Facebook handles 50 billion photos from its user base [43].
- As of August 2012, *Google* was handling roughly 100 billion searches per month [44].
- *Oracle NoSQL Database* has been tested to pass the 1 million ops/sec mark with eight shards and proceeded to hit 1.2 million ops/sec with 10 shards [45].
- **Retail:** Walmart handles more than 1 million customer transactions every hour, which are imported into databases estimated to contain more than 2.5 PB (2,560 TB) of data— the equivalent of 167 times the information contained in all the books in the U.S. Library of Congress [46].

Real Estate

Windermere Real Estate uses anonymous GPS (global positioning system) signals from nearly 100 million drivers to help new home buyers determine their typical drive times to and from work throughout various times of the day [47].

Science and Research

- Decoding the *human genome* originally took 10 years to process; now it can be achieved in less than a day. The DNA sequencers have divided the sequencing cost by 10,000 in the last 10 years, which is 100 times cheaper than the reduction in cost predicted by *Moore's Law* [48].

- The *NASA* Center for Climate Simulation (NCCS) stores 32 PB of climate observations and simulations on the Discover supercomputing cluster [49].

- Google's DNAstack compiles and organizes DNA samples of genetic data from around the world to identify diseases and other medical defects.

Fundamental Concepts in Data Visualization

Data visualization is an essential part of data analysis. Different approaches to data analysis include:

1. Data visualization (commonly used graphical techniques are histograms, scatterplots, surface plots, area plots, time-series plots, tree maps, and others described in Chapter 3)
2. Statistical methods that include inference procedures, such as estimation, hypothesis tests, analysis of variance, regression analysis, and so on
3. *Data mining* (*association mining*)
4. Data analytics including predictive and prescriptive analytics tools
5. *Machine learning* methods (*clustering*, *classification*, *decision trees*, etc.)

Among these approaches, visual data analysis is the most powerful and easy to use and comprehend. It relies on the cognitive skills of the analysts, and enables one to visualize the features and patterns in large amounts of data. Current data visualization software can process vast amount of data quickly and create different visualizations of the same data set that allows discovery of the hidden patterns and simultaneous views of the process (e.g., analysis of online order processing data). The graphics in the visualization software are simple and most of them can be learned fairly quickly unless in-depth analysis is required. Later in this chapter, we provide examples of simple graphs that are fairly easy to create and interpret. Sometimes, for in-depth and analytical analysis, inferential statistical tools including estimation theory, hypothesis testing, analysis of variance, and others are required. This requires knowledge of statistical methods beyond simple graphical analysis. For simple visualizations, the analyst does not have to learn any sophisticated methods or statistical theories to be able to interpret the graphs.

Different Forms of Data Visualization

Data visualization is closely related to *information graphics, information visualization, scientific visualization, exploratory data* analysis, and *statistical graphics*. In the new millennium, data visualization has become an active area of research, teaching, and development.

Information visualization or information graphics or infographics are graphic representations of *information, data,* or *knowledge* intended to present information quickly and clearly [50][51]. They can improve cognition by utilizing graphics to enhance the human visual system's ability to see patterns and trends [52][53]. Similar pursuits are *information visualization, data visualization, statistical graphics, information design,* or *information architecture* [51].

Characteristics of Effective Graphical Displays

In his 1983 book *The Visual Display of Quantitative Information, Edward Tufte* defines "graphical displays" and principles for effective graphical display in the following passage:

> Excellence in statistical graphics consists of complex ideas communicated with clarity, precision and efficiency. Graphical displays should:
>
> (1) show the data, (2) induce the viewer to think about the substance rather than about methodology, graphic design, the technology of graphic production or something else, (3) avoid distorting what the data has to say, (4) present many numbers in a small space, (5) make large data sets coherent, (6) encourage the eye to compare different pieces of data, (7) reveal the data at

several levels of detail, from a broad overview to the fine structure, (8) serve a reasonably clear purpose: description, exploration, tabulation or decoration, (9) be closely integrated with the statistical and verbal descriptions of a data set.

Graphics *reveal* data. Indeed graphics can be more precise and revealing than conventional statistical computations.[54]

Quantitative Messages Conveyed by Simple Data Visualization

Author Stephen Few described eight types of quantitative messages that users may attempt to understand or communicate from a set of data and the associated graphs used to communicate the message:

1. Time-series: a single variable is captured over a period of time, such as the unemployment rate over a 10-year period. A *line chart* may be used to demonstrate the trend.
2. Ranking: categorical subdivisions are ranked in ascending or descending order, such as a ranking of sales performance (the *measure*) by sales persons (the *category*, with each salesperson a *categorical subdivision*) during a single period. A *bar chart* may be used to show the comparison across the sales persons.
3. Part-to-whole: categorical subdivisions are measured as a ratio to the whole (i.e., a percentage out of 100 percent). A *pie chart* or bar chart can show the comparison of ratios, such as the market share represented by competitors in a market.
4. Deviation: categorical subdivisions are compared against a reference, such as a comparison of actual versus budget expenses for several departments of a business for a given time period. A bar chart can show comparison of the actual versus the reference amount.
5. Frequency distribution: it shows the number of observations of a particular variable for a given interval, such as the number of years in which the stock market return is between intervals such as 0 and 10 percent, 11 and 20 percent, and so on. A *histogram*, a type of bar chart, may be used for this analysis. A *boxplot* helps visualize key statistics about the distribution, such as median, quartiles, outliers, and so on.

6. Correlation: comparison between observations represented by two variables (X, Y) to determine if they tend to move in the same or opposite directions. For example, plotting unemployment (X) and inflation (Y) for a sample of months. A *scatterplot* is typically used for this message.

7. Nominal comparison: comparing categorical subdivisions in no particular order, such as the sales volume by product code. A bar chart may be used for this comparison.

8. Geographic or geospatial: comparison of a variable across a map or layout, such as the unemployment rate by state or the number of people on the various floors of a building. A *cartogram* is a typical graphic used [55][56].

Analysts reviewing a set of data may consider whether some or all of the messages and graphic types shown earlier are applicable to their task and audience. The process of trial and error to identify meaningful relationships and messages in the data is part of *exploratory data analysis*.

Software Tools for Data Visualization

With the progression of technology came the progression of data visualization, starting with hand-drawn visualizations and evolving into more technical applications—including interactive designs leading to software visualization [57]. Programs like *SAS*, *SOFA*, *R*, *Minitab*, and more allow for data visualization in the field of statistics. Other data visualization applications, are more focused and unique to individuals, programming languages such as D3, Python, and JavaScript help to make the visualization of quantitative data a possibility.

Terminology for Data Visualization

Data visualization involves specific terminology, some of which is derived from statistics. For example, author Stephen Few defines two types of data, which are used in combination to support a meaningful analysis or visualization:

- Categorical: text labels describing the nature of the data, such as "Name" or "Age." This term also covers qualitative (nonnumerical) data.
- Quantitative: numerical measures, such as "25" to represent the age in years.

Types of Information Displays

Two primary types of *information displays* are *data visualization* and *information visualization*.

Data visualization uses mainly tables, charts, and graphs.

- A *table* contains quantitative data organized into rows and columns with categorical labels. It is primarily used to look up specific values. In the previous example, the table might have categorical column labels representing the name (a *qualitative variable*) and age (a *quantitative variable*), with each row of data representing one person (the sampled *experimental unit* or *category subdivision*).
- A *graph* is primarily used to show relationships among data and portrays values encoded as *visual objects* (e.g., lines, bars, or points). Numerical values are displayed within an area delineated by one or more *axes*. These axes provide *scales* (quantitative and categorical) used to label and assign values to the visual objects. Many graphs are also referred to as *charts* [58].
- *Information visualization* uses flow diagrams, flow process charts, value stream maps, and cause-and-effect diagrams to display the information.

Data Visualization Software Applications

One of the most effective ways of visualizing big data is to create visuals that can show different views of the data. A number of charts and graphs of the business process can be created using dashboards that can tell the story using graphical displays. As we know, the data and numbers alone are not effective in revealing the characteristics in data. It is hard to see the trends and patterns in the data without creating visuals. In other words, data alone don't always tell the full story. Data visualization, visual analytics, and business intelligence software should be used to tell the full story. Data visualization and business intelligence software can create interactive and customizable dashboards that allow one to measure performance in real time. This software provides drag and drop design where data can be easily added and removed so that visualization can be added and arranged in different ways. The built-in design also allows performing simple to advanced calculations.

With ever increasing demand for managing and handling big data, the data visualization and business intelligence software are critical in visualizing and analyzing data from across the organization to gain valuable insight and to make accurate and timely decisions. Figures 5.1 and 5.2 are examples of simple dashboards showing different scenarios of the same data collected from an online ordering process of a business. These dashboards are very helpful in simultaneously visualizing key business performance that can be used in effective and timely decision making.

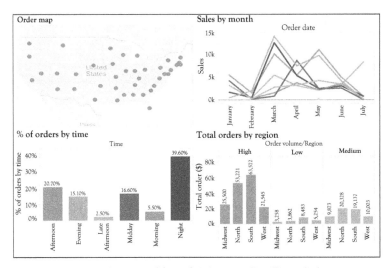

Figure 5.1 Example of Dashboard (1) using Big Data Software Tableau

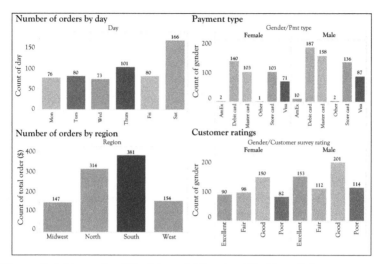

Figure 5.2 Example of Dashboard (2) using Big Data Software Tableau

Summary

This chapter provided an introduction to big data, data visualization, and visual analytics. Data visualization is a form of visual communication that involves exploring huge amount of data using charts and graphs and also flowcharts and diagrams. These visuals are very helpful in drawing conclusions and making effective decisions. Data visualization makes complex and big data understandable. Examples and applications of big data in different areas including health care, government, manufacturing, education, and others were presented. Some fundamental concepts in data visualization, forms of data visualization, and the characteristics of effective graphical displays were discussed. Software tools currently available in the big data area—and some dashboards created using one of the big data software—Tableau—were presented.

CHAPTER 6

Basic Analytics Tools: Describing Data Numerically—Concepts and Computer Analysis

Chapter Highlights

Data Exploration Using Statistics to Summarize Data: Chapter Highlights

Numerical Methods of Describing and Analyzing Data

Measures of Central Tendency

    Mean or the Average/ *Weighted Mean*

    Median

    Mode

    Comparing Mean, Median, and Mode

Measures of Position: Percentiles and Quartiles

    Calculating Percentiles and Quartiles

Measures of Variation

    What Does the Variation or Dispersion Tell Us?

Different Measures of Variation or Dispersion

    (1) Range

    (2) Variance

    (3) Standard Deviation

    (4) Coefficient of Variation

    (5) Interquartile Range

    Calculating the Sample Variance, s^2

    Summary of Formulas for Sample and Population

    Describing Data: A Case

    Different Statistics Used to Describe the Data

Statistics Based on Ordered Values
Statistics Based on Averages
Describing Distributions (Symmetrical, Bell-Shaped or
Normal)
Relationship Between the Mean and Standard Deviation
Chebyshev's Theorem
Empirical Rule
Application of the Empirical Rule
Exploratory Data Analysis
Box Plot
Elements of a Box Plot
Interpreting Box Plots
Outliers: Detecting Outliers Using Box Plots and Z-Scores
Summary

Data Exploration Using Statistics to Summarize Data

This chapter deals with the basic statistical tools of analytics. The primary objective of this chapter is to enable you to master the techniques of describing data using numerical methods, perform analyses and use these methods to compare and draw meaningful conclusions from data. All these techniques use computer software in real world.

Numerical Methods of Describing and Analyzing Data

Numerical methods include several statistical measures that are used to describe the data. Earlier, graphical techniques and their importance in describing and summarizing data were discussed in detail. This chapter deals with the measures that are used to describe and summarize numerical variables. Although visual representation of data such as, the charts and graphs are very helpful in summarizing, visualizing the pattern, and drawing conclusions from the data; in many cases, additional numerical measures are needed to describe the data. In this chapter, we will investigate the numerical measures that involve computations to describe, summarize, and draw meaningful conclusions from the data. We will also discuss computer applications and data analysis concepts in this chapter.

The numerical methods of describing data can be divided into following categories: (1) measures of central tendency or measures of location, (2) measures of position, (3) measures of variation or dispersion, and (4) the measures of shape. We will discuss all these measures here.

Measures of Central Tendency

The common measures of central tendency are:

1. Mean
2. Median
3. Mode

The mean or the average is a statistical constant which enable us to comprehend the significance of the whole. It provides an idea about the concentration of the data in the central part of the distribution. The requirements for the ideal measures of central tendency are that they should be (1) uniquely defined, (2) based on all observations, (3) affected as little as possible by fluctuations in sampling, and (4) suitable for further mathematical treatment.

The median is the value of the variable that divides the data into two equal parts, such that half of the value lies above the median and the other half below it.

The mode is the value of the variable which occurs most frequently, or repeated the maximum number of times in a data set. We will discuss these in more detail in sections that follow.

Mean or the Average

The mean or the average is commonly used to obtain a typical representation of a group as a whole. When we refer to the "average" of something, we are talking about the arithmetic mean. For example, the average grade of students in a statistics course, average life of a car battery, and so on.

The mean of a data set is sum of the values divided by the number of observations. The mean of n observations $x_1, x_2, \ldots, x_n$ is given by

$$\text{Mean} = \frac{x_1 + x_2 + x_3 + \ldots\ldots + x_n}{n}$$

or,

$$\text{Mean} = \frac{\sum all\ values}{n} = \frac{\sum x}{n}$$

In the aforementioned formula, x_1 is the first value of the variable, x_2 is the second value and so on. The total number of observations is n and $\sum$ is the summation sign. Suppose we collected data on the hourly wage for five employees of a company. Then the wage is a *variable*. If the wages are $12, $13, $10, $15, and $10 then x_1 is 12, which is the first data point or the first value of variable, x_2 is 13 or the second value of the variable, and so on. To calculate the average wage, we would sum all the values and divide it by 5, the total number of observations. Thus, the mean or the average wage would be

$$\text{Mean} = \frac{12 + 13 + 10 + 15 + 10}{5} = \frac{60}{5} = \$12$$

In the aforementioned example, we collected data on only five employees. We call this data a sample data. If we collect data on all the employees in that company, such data will be called a population data. A sample is part of a population and statistical analysis mostly relies on taking samples. The reason why samples are taken for statistical analysis is because collecting and analyzing the population data would be very time consuming and expensive.

It is important to distinguish whether the summary statistic, such as the mean is being calculated from a sample data or a population data. The formulas for the sample and population mean are given as follows. *Sample Mean Population Mean*

$$\bar{x} = \frac{\sum x_i}{n} \tag{6.1}$$

$$\mu = \frac{\sum x_i}{N} \qquad (6.2)$$

Example 1

The number of accidents for the past six months on a particular highway is given in the following.

5   8   10   7   10   14

The sample mean $\bar{x}$ is calculated as

$$\bar{x} = \frac{\sum x}{n} = \frac{5+8+10+7+10+14}{6} = 9$$

The aforementioned calculation shows that the average number of accidents was 9. The mean can be interpreted in the following ways:

- It provides a single number presenting the whole data set.
- It gives us the significance of the whole.
- It is unique because every data set has only one mean.
- It is useful for comparing different data sets in terms of the average.

Disadvantages of Mean

The mean can be affected by extreme values (extreme values are very high or very low values in a data set that may be difficult to detect in a large data set). Suppose we calculate the sample mean for the following data:

$$\bar{x} = \frac{5.2+5.4+5.7+5.8+6.0+5.9+12.0}{7} = 6.57$$

In the aforementioned data, the value 12 is an extreme value. The mean without this extreme value, would be

$$\bar{x} = \frac{5.2+5.4+5.7+5.8+6.0+5.9}{6} = 5.67$$

This provides a better representation of data.

Weighted Mean

In calculating the mean using the earlier formula, each observation in the data has equal weight. In some cases, each observation in the data may not be given the same weight and therefore, the mean cannot be calculated by taking the simple average as shown previously by the sample mean formula. When the data values cannot be weighted equally, we calculate a weighted mean of the data by providing different weight or importance to different data values. The weighted mean is calculated using the following formula:

$$\bar{x} = \frac{\sum w_i x_i}{\sum w_i}$$

Where, x_i is the ith observation and W_i is the weight given to the ith observation.

Example 2

One of the common applications of weighted average is the calculation of the grade point average (GPA) where each letter grade is given a different value. For most colleges and universities the letter grades usually are based on similar data values. Suppose your college uses the following values for the letter grades:

A(4),   A– (3.7),   B+   (3.3),   B (3.0),   B–   (2.7), C   (2.0), D(1) , F   (0)

Suppose you have completed 70 credit hours of course work and earned an A grade for 18 credit hours, A– for 21 credit hours, B+ for 28 credit hours, and a B for 3 credit hours. What is your GPA?

Solution: The GPA can be calculated using the weighted average as shown as follows.

Grade, x_i	Weight, w_i
A (4)	18
A– (3.7)	21
B+ (3.3)	28
B (3.0)	3
	70 Credits

The weighted average,

$$\bar{x} = \frac{\sum w_i x_i}{\sum w_i} = \frac{18(4) + 21(3.7) + 28(3.3) + 3(3)}{18 + 21 + 28 + 3} = 3.587 \approx 3.6$$

Median

The *median* is another measure of central tendency. The median is the middle value of a data set when the data are arranged in increasing (or decreasing) order. The median divides the data into two equal parts, such that half of the values lie above the median and the other half below it. The median is the value that measures the central item in the data. For the ungrouped data (data not grouped into a frequency distribution) the median is calculated based on whether the number of observations is odd or even.

Calculating Median When the Number of Observations Is Odd

If the number of observations is odd, the median can be calculated by

- Arranging the data in increasing order.
- Locating the middle value after the values have been arranged in ascending order of magnitude.

Note that there is a distinct median when the number of observations is odd. Unlike the mean, the median is not affected by extreme values.

Median When the Number of Observations Is Even

When the number of observations is even, there are two middle values, and the median is obtained by taking the arithmetic mean of the middle terms.

Example 3

Suppose we have the following observations arranged in increasing order:

1	2	3	4	5	6	7
8.2	8.3	8.9	9.6	9.8	10.2	12.0

The number of observations is 7 ($n=7$) which is odd therefore, the middle value or the median is the fourth value which is 9.6.

Suppose the following data are the annual incomes of eight employees of a manufacturing company for the past year. Find the median.

1	2	3	4	5	6	7	8
70	62	60	45	40	56	38	35

The number of observations is: n=8 (even)

• Arrange the data in increasing order

1	2	3	4	5	6	7	8
35	38	40	45	56	60	62	70

• The location of the median for even observations is given by

$$\frac{n+1}{2} = \frac{8+1}{2} = 4.5$$

(6.3)

Therefore, the median is the average of 4th and 5th values

$$\text{Median} = \frac{45+56}{2} = 50.5$$

This means that 50.5 is the median income. Note that when the number of observations is even, there is no distinct median. The advantage of the median is that it is not affected by extreme values in a data set and is easy to understand and calculate. The disadvantage is that in case of even number of observations, the median cannot be calculated exactly. It can only be estimated by taking the mean of two middle terms. The other problem with the median is that it is the average of positions, and the data must be arranged in a data array before we can calculate the median.

Mode

The mode is the value that occurs most frequently in a set of observations. In other words, it is the value that is repeated most often in the data set.

Sometimes chance causes a single often-repeated value to be the most frequent value in the data set.

Example 4

The following data represent the number of hours of use of personal computer per day by a sample 20 employees at work:

3	2	3	4	3	0	1	3	5	2	3
4	3	1	1	3	2	1	3	3		

The mode for this data is three hours because this value is repeated the maximum number of times.

Mode=three hours

If you calculate the average for the data, you will find,

$$\bar{x} = \frac{\sum x}{n} = \frac{50}{20} = 2.5\,hours$$

The mode of three hours tells us that the usage is higher than the average of 2.5 hours. It also tells us that three is the most frequent number of hours of usage, but it fails to tell us what values are above or below it.

Advantages of the Mode

- It is easy to calculate; in some cases, it can be located by inspection.
- It is not affected by extreme values.

Disadvantages

- It is not always possible to find a unique mode in a data set. Some data may have more than one mode. If the data has a unique mode, then we have a *unimodal* data. If a data set has two modes then it is *bi-modal*. In case of more than two modes, the data is *multimodal*.
- Sometimes there may not be any mode in the data as none of the values repeat or there may be cases where several values repeat same number of time. In cases, where there are several modes in the data, the mode is a useless measure. If the

data set contains two, three or many modes, interpretation becomes difficult.

Comparing Mean, Median, and Mode

Note that we calculate the mean, median, mode, and other statistics from the data in order to characterize the data. If you have 500 observations, it is hard to draw any conclusion or make comparison. The mean, median, and mode are some of the simple statistics we calculate to draw meaningful conclusions from the data. Therefore, it is important to decide which measure of central tendency best describes the data (mean, median, or mode).

> *If the data are symmetrical; the mean, median, and mode are all centrally located and they have the same or approximately same value.*

A symmetrical distribution is also known as a bell-shaped or normal distribution. In a symmetrical distribution, if a vertical line is drawn from the peak to the base of the curve, it will divide the shape into two equal parts which are mirror images of each other.

In case of skewed data (skewness means the lack of symmetry), the mean, median, and mode are not located at the same place. A distribution (shape) can be right skewed or left skewed. *The right skewed distribution* is tailed to the right and is also known as *positively skewed*. A *left skewed distribution* is tailed to the left and is also known as *negatively skewed*. In a right skewed or positively skewed data,

Mean > Median, and

Mean > Mode

Figure 6.1(a) and (b) show a right skewed or positively skewed and a left or negatively skewed distribution. In a left skewed or negatively skewed data,

Mean < Median, and

Mean < Mode

Note that when the distribution is skewed negatively or positively, the *median* is always midway between the mean and the mode. Therefore, median is often used to describe a skewed data and is the best measure for central tendency whenever data are skewed.

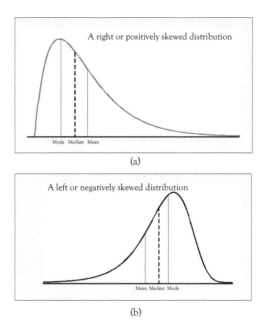

Figure 6.1 **(a) A right or positively skewed (b) A left or negatively skewed distribution**

Thus, if you calculate the mean, median, and mode from a set of data, you can tell if the data are symmetrical or skewed by comparing the values of these measures. Some data such as, the age or income are often skewed. Therefore, when drawing conclusion from skewed data, we compare the median age or the median income.

Measures of Position: Percentiles and Quartiles

Quantitative data are sometimes summarized in terms of percentiles. A percentile is a point below which a stated percentage or proportion of observations lie. Quartiles are special percentiles which divide the observations into groups of successive size, each containing 25 percent of the data points. The quartiles are denoted by Q_1: the first quartile or 25th percentile; Q_2: the second quartile or 50th percentile (which is also the median); and Q_3: the third quartile or 75th percentile. Another measure calculated using the quartiles is *interquartile range* which is the difference between the third quartile and the first quartile and encompasses the middle 50 percent of the values. One very useful data summary called *the five measure summary* provides a visual display of the data in form of a plot known as the *box plot*. This is a plot of the minimum and maximum values and three quartiles, Q_1, Q_2, and Q_3. The box plot shows the data extremes, the range, the median, the quartiles, and the interquartile range (IQR).

A percentile tells us how the data values are spread out over the interval from the smallest value to the largest value.

> *The pth percentile of a data set is a value, such that at least p percent of the values are less than or equal to this value, and at least (100-p) percent of the values are greater than or equal to this value.*

If a score on a SAT test states that a student is at 85th percentile, it means that 85 percent who took the test had scores at or below this value and 15 percent of those who took the test scored higher than this value. The percentile value provides us a comparison in relation to other values.

The quartiles divide the data into four parts. For a large data set, it is often desirable to divide the data into four parts. This can be done by calculating the quartile. Note that

Q_1 = 1st quartile or 25th percentile
Q_2 = 2nd quartile or 50th percentile or the median
Q_3 = 3rd quartile or 75th percentile

The first quartile or Q_1 is the value such that 25 percent of the observations are below Q_1 and 75 percent of the values are above Q_1. The other quartiles can be interpreted in a similar way. Using the following formula, we can determine the percentile and quartile for any data set.

Calculating Percentiles and Quartiles

To find a percentile or quartile:

- Arrange the data in increasing order
- Find the location of the percentile using the following formula

$$L_p = (n+1)\frac{P}{100}$$

(6.4)

where, L_p = location of the percentile, n = total number of observations, P = desired percentile

Example 5

Find the median, the first quartile, and the third quartile for the data in Table 6.1.

Solution: Note that the number of observations is 15 (n=15). First, arrange the data in increasing order. The sorted values are shown in Table 6.2.

Table 6.3 shows the descriptive statistics for the data in Table 6.1 calculated using MINITAB. Note that when descriptive statistics are calculated for a set of data using MINITAB, it calculates the median, the first quartile Q1, and the third quartile Q3, among other statistics. Here, we will verify the results of the median or the 50th percentile (also known as Q2), Q1, and Q3 as reported by MINITAB.

Table 6.1 Data for example problem

2038	1758	1721	1637	2097	2047	2205	1787	2287	1940	2311	2054	2406
1471	1460											

Table 6.2 Sorted data

Sorted data												
1460	1471	1637	1721	1758	1787	1940	2038	2047	2054	2097	2205	2287
2311	2406											

Table 6.3 Descriptive statistics using MINITAB

Descriptive statistics calculations using MINITAB						
Variable	N	Mean	Median	TrMean	StDev	SE Mean
Data	15	1947.9	2038.0	1950.2	298.8	77.1
Variable		Minimum	Maximum	Q1	Q3	
Data		1460.0	2406.0	1721.0	2205.0	

(a) Calculate the median or Q2 (50th percentile) using equation (6.4) and compare it to the median calculated by MINITAB in Table 6.3.

First, calculate the position of the median or Q2 using equation (6.4) as shown in the following.

$$L_p = (n+1)\frac{P}{100} = 16\left(\frac{50}{100}\right) = 8$$

Therefore, the 8th value in the sorted data (Table 6.2) is the median or Q2. This value is 2,038. Therefore, *Median=2,038*

This result is the same as the value of the median in Table 6.3.

(b) Calculate the first quartile or Q1 (25th percentile) using equation (6.4) and compare it

to the Q1 value calculated by MINITAB in Table 6.3.

$$L_p = (n+1)\frac{P}{100} = 16\left(\frac{25}{100}\right) = 4$$

Calculate the position of Q1 using equation (6.4) as shown in the following.

The 4th value in the sorted data (Table 6.3) is Q1. This value is 1,721. Therefore,

Q1=1,721

(c) Calculate the third quartile or Q3 (75th percentile) using equation (6.4) and compare it to the

$$L_p = (n+1)\frac{P}{100} = 16\left(\frac{75}{100}\right) = 12$$

Q3 value calculated by MINITAB in Table 6.3.

The 12th value in the sorted data is Q3. This value is 2,205. Therefore,

Q3=2,205

The values of Q1, Q2 (the median), and Q3 calculated using equation (6.4) agrees with the computer result in Table 6.3.

Example 6

The data in Table 6.4 shows the monthly income of 20 part-time employees of a company. Find the median, the first quartile, and the third quartile values of the income data. Table 6.5 shows the sorted values from Table 6.4.

Table 6.6 shows the descriptive statistics for the data in Table 6.4. This table shows the median, first quartile, and the third quartile values. We have explained earlier how to obtain these values using the percentile formula.

Note that the number of observations, $n=20$.

The median or Q2 (50th percentile) is located at

$$L_p = (n+1)\frac{P}{100} = 21\left(\frac{50}{100}\right) = 10.5$$

This means that the median is located half way between the 10th and 11th value, or the average of the 10th and 11th value in the sorted data. This value is $(1,940+2,038)/2=1,989$.

Table 6.4 Monthly income

Monthly income							
2038	1758	1721	1637	2097	2047	2205	1787
2287	1940	2311	2054	2406	1471	1460	1500
2250	1650	2100	1850				

Table 6.5 Sorted income data

Sorted data (read row-wise)							
1460	1471	1500	1637	1650	1721	1758	1787
1850	1940	2038	2047	2054	2097	2100	2205
2250	2287	2311	2406				

Table 6.6 Descriptive statistics of income data using MINITAB

Calculations using MINITAB						
Variable	N	Mean	Median	TrMean	StDev	SE Mean
Data	20	1928.5	1989.0	1927.9	295.2	66.0
Variable		Minimum	Maximum	Q1	Q3	
Data		1460.0	2406.0	1667.8	2178.8	

Therefore, *Median or Q2=1,989*

The first Quartile (Q1) or 25th percentile is located at

$$L_p = (n+1)\frac{P}{100} = 21\left(\frac{25}{100}\right) = 5.25$$

Therefore, Q1 is the 5th value in the sorted data, plus 0.25 times the difference between the 5th and the 6th value, which is 1,650+(.25) (1,721–1,650)=1,667.75 or,

Q1=1,667.75 or 1,667.8

The 3rd Quartile (Q3) or 75th percentile is located at

$$L_p = (n+1)\frac{P}{100} = 21\left(\frac{75}{100}\right) = 15.75$$

Thus, Q3 is the 15th value in the sorted data, plus 0.75 times the difference between the 15th and the 16th value, which is 2,100+(.75) (2,205–2,100)=2,178.75

Therefore,

Q3=2,178.75 or 2,178.8

The calculated values of the median, Q1, and Q3 are the same as in Table 6.6.

Measures of Variation

The measures of central tendency provide an idea about the concentration of observations about the central part of distribution. If we know the mean alone, we cannot form a complete idea about the distribution. Consider the following sets of data and the mean calculated from them.

7, 8, 9, 10, 11: the mean, $\bar{x} = \dfrac{\sum x}{n} = \dfrac{45}{5} = 9.0$

3, 6, 9, 12, 15: the mean, $\bar{x} = 9.0$

1, 5, 9, 13, 17: the mean $\bar{x} = 9.0$

The mean of all the aforementioned three sets of observations is 9.0. Knowing just the mean does not describe the data fully. The previous examples show that any five observations whose sum is 45 will have a mean of 9. This does not tell us anything about the variation in the observations and therefore, does not provide a complete description of the data.

The measures of central tendency (mean, median, and mode) are not sufficient to give us a complete description of the data. They must be supported by other measures. These measures are the *measures of variation* or *measures of dispersion*. They tell us about the variation or dispersion of the data values around the average. We may have two or more sets of data all having the same average, but their spread or variability may be different. This is shown in Figures 6.2 and 6.3. Figure 6.2 shows that the data set A and B have the same mean but different variations. In this figure, curve B has less spread or variability than curve A. The more variation the data has, the more spread out the curve will be. We may also have a case where two sets of data have the same variation but different means. You can see this in Figure 6.3.

If we measure only the mean of different data, we miss other important characteristics. Mean, median, and mode tell us only part of what we need to know about the characteristic of the data. In order to better

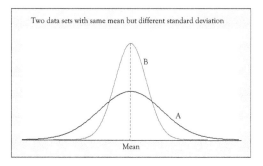

Figure 6.2 Data sets A and B with same mean but different variation

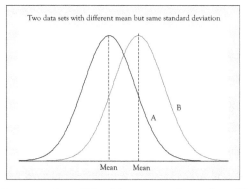

Figure 6.3 Data sets A and B with same variation but different mean

analyze and understand the data, we must also measure its dispersion; that is, its spread or variability.

What does the variation or dispersion tell us?

- It gives us additional information that enables us to judge the reliability of the measure of central tendency. If the data has more spread or variation, the central location is less representative of the data as a whole than it would be for data that is more closely centered around the mean.
- Dispersion or the variation is often used to compare two or more sets of data. In statistical quality control, one of the major objectives is to measure and reduce variability. This is done by extracting data from the process at different stages or time intervals, and analyzing the data by different means, in order to measure and reduce variation. As the variation in the product is reduced, the product becomes more consistent.

Just like the measures of central tendency, there are different measures of dispersion or variation. The next section explains the different ways of measuring the dispersion or variation in data.

Different Measures of Variation or Dispersion

The variability in the data is measured using the following measures. These are known as the *measures of variation.*

1. Range
2. Variance
3. Standard Deviation
4. Coefficient of Variation
5. Interquartile Range

(1) Range

Range is the simplest measure of variability. It is the difference between the maximum (largest) and minimum (smallest) value in the data set.

$$Range = (Maximum\ Value - Minimum\ Value) \qquad (6.5)$$

Range is easy to calculate and understand but its use is limited.

- The range takes into account only the largest and the smallest value and ignores the other observations.
- It is affected by extreme values.
- It takes into account only two values that can change drastically from sample to sample.
- This measure of variation is not suggested for large data set.

Example 7

The data in Table 6.7 shows the monthly salaries (in dollars) for 15 employees of a company. Calculate the range.

Table 6.7 Monthly salary

2038	1758	1721	1637	2097	2047	2205	1787
2287	1940	2311	2054	2406	1471	1460	

Solution: It is easier to calculate the range if the data are sorted. The sorted data from Table 6.7 are shown as follows.

1460   1471   1637   1721   1758   1787   1940   2038
2047   2054   2097   2205   2287   2311   2406

The largest value in the data is 2,406 and the smallest value is 1,460. Therefore,

Range=(2,406–1,460)=946 dollars

Note that a large range indicates a large variation.

(2) Variance

The variance measures the average of the squared deviation of the values from a fixed point, mean ($\bar{x}$) and can be calculated for both the sample and the population data. The variance calculated from a sample data is called the sample variance; whereas the variance calculated from the population data is known as the population variance. It is important to note the distinction between the sample and the population variance. They are denoted by different symbols, have the same concept, but slightly differ in values.

Sample Variance (Denoted by s^2)

Sample variance is the sum of the squared differences between each of the observations and the mean. It is the average of squared distances. Suppose we have n number of observations $x_1, x_2, x_3, ..., x_n$ then the variance, s^2 is

$$s^2 = \frac{(x_1 - \bar{x})^2 + (x_2 - \bar{x})^2 + ... + (x_n - \bar{x})^2}{n-1}$$

or,

$$s^2 = \frac{\sum (x_i - \bar{x})^2}{n-1} \qquad (6.6)$$

Where,

$\bar{x}$ = sample mean

n = sample size or number of observations

x_i = ith value of the random variable x (note that x_1 is the first value of the data point, x_2 is the second value of the data point, and so on).

$\sum (x_i - \bar{x})^2$ is the sum of all squared differences between each of x_i values and the mean.

Another formula to calculate the sample variance
In equation (6.7),

$$s^2 = \frac{\sum x^2 - \frac{\left(\sum x\right)^2}{n}}{n-1} \qquad (6.7)$$

$\sum x^2$ is the sum of the squared values of the variable, x and

$\sum x$ is the sum of the values of the variable, x

Mathematically, both equations (6.6) and (6.7) are identical and provide the same result. Equation (6.7) is computationally easier than equation (6.6) for manual calculation because the first equation requires calculating the mean from the data, then subtracting the mean from each observation, squaring the values, and finally adding them. This process is tedious for large data set. The second equation simplifies the calculation

Calculating the Sample Variance, s^2

To calculate the variance using the aforementioned equation (6.6):

- Calculate the mean of the data
- Obtain the difference between each observation and the mean
- Square each difference
- Add the squared differences
- Divide the sum by $(n-1)$

Example 8

The following data represents the price of certain item in dollars

5, 8, 10, 7, 10, 14

Calculate the variance using equation (6.6). Note that $n = 6$ (the number of observations)

Solution: First, calculate the sample mean using the following formula.

$$\bar{x} = \frac{\sum x}{n} = \frac{5+8+10+7+10+14}{6} = 9$$

Next, subtract each observation from the mean, square, and add the squared values. The calculations can be performed using the following table.

x_i	$(x_i - \bar{x})^2$
5	$(5-9)^2 = 16$
8	$(8-9)^2 = 1$
10	$(10-9)^2 = 1$
7	$(7-9)^2 = 4$
10	$(10-9)^2 = 1$
14	$(14-9)^2 = 25$
	$\sum (x_i - \bar{x})^2 = 48$

The sample variance can now be calculated, using equation (6.6) as

$$s^2 = \frac{\sum (x_i - \bar{x})^2}{n-1} = \frac{48}{5} = 9.6\,(dollars)^2$$

Note that the unit in which the data is measured (dollar in this case) is also squared because we are taking each dollar value in the data, subtracting the mean from it, and then squaring it. This results in squared units which is a difficult configuration to interpret. This is the reason we take the square root of the variance. The value that is obtained by taking the square root of the variance is known as the *standard deviation*. Usually, we use the standard deviation to measure and compare the variability of two or more sets of data, not the variance. We will discuss the standard deviation in a later section. Before that, we will demonstrate the calculation of variance using the previous equation (6.7).

Calculating the variance using equation (6.7)
The following example shows the calculation of variance using equation (6.7). This equation is given by

$$s^2 = \frac{\sum x^2 - \frac{\left(\sum x\right)^2}{n}}{n-1}$$

The calculation of variance using the aforementioned is explained in the following table.

x_i	x_i^2
5	25
8	64
10	100
7	49
10	100
14	196
$\sum x_i = 54$	$\sum x_i^2 = 534$

Using equation (6.7), the variance

$$s^2 = \frac{\sum x^2 - \frac{\left(\sum x\right)^2}{n}}{n-1} = \frac{534 - \frac{(54)^2}{6}}{5} = \frac{48}{5} = 9.6$$

The variance obtained by this method is same as using equation (6.6). Note the following features of variance:

- Variance can never be negative
- If all the values in the data set are the same, the variance and standard deviation are zero, indicating no variability

- Usually, no random phenomena will ever have the same measured values therefore, it is important to know the variation in the data.

1. *Standard Deviation*

The sample standard deviation (denoted by s) is calculated by taking the square root of the variance. The standard deviation can be calculated using the following formulas.

$$s = \sqrt{s^2} = \sqrt{\frac{\sum (x_i - \bar{x})^2}{n-1}}$$

or

$$s = \sqrt{s^2} = \sqrt{\frac{\sum x^2 - \frac{\left(\sum x\right)^2}{n}}{n-1}} \qquad (6.8)$$

Example 9

Calculate the standard deviation of the data in Example 8.

Solution: To calculate the standard deviation, we first calculate the variance using either equation (6.6) or (6.7) shown earlier. Using the variance calculated in Example 8, the standard deviation can be calculated as

$$s = \sqrt{\frac{\sum (x_i - \bar{x})^2}{n-1}} = \sqrt{\frac{48}{5}} = 3.1$$

The sample standard deviation, $s = 3.1$ dollars

What do the variance (s^2) and the standard deviation (s) tell us?

The variance and standard deviation measure the average deviation (or the scatter) around the mean. The variance is the average of squared distances from the mean. In calculating the variance, the computation results in squared units, such as dollar squared, inch squared, and so on. This makes the interpretation difficult. Therefore, for practical purposes we calculate the standard deviation by taking the square root of the variance. Taking the square root of the variance results in the original unit of data (it is no more dollars squared or inch squared, but dollars or inches). In other words, the variance is the measure of variation affected by the units of measurement; whereas the standard deviation is measured in the same unit as the data. In Example 9, $s = 3.1$ dollars tells us that the average deviation of the price is 3.1 dollars.

Why square the deviation?
In the formula for the variance [see equation (6.6)], $(x_i - \bar{x})$ is squared. That is,

$$(x_i - \bar{x})^2$$

If the values are not squared the result would be zero. That is,

$$\sum (x_i - \bar{x}) = 0$$

Note: The more "spread out" or dispersed the data, the larger will be the range, the variance, and the standard deviation. The more centered the data are around the mean, the smaller will be the range, the variance, and the standard deviation.

(4) *Coefficient of Variation (CV)*

The coefficient of variation (CV) is a relative measure of dispersion expressed as percentage. It tells us how large the standard deviation is in relation to the mean. It is calculated using the following formula:

Sample coefficient of variation (CV)

$$CV = \frac{\text{Standard Deviation}}{\text{Mean}} * 100\% \ or,$$

$$CV = \frac{s}{\bar{x}} * 100\% \qquad\qquad (6.9)$$

Population coefficient of variation (CV)

$$CV = \frac{\sigma}{\mu} * 100\% \qquad\qquad (6.10)$$

Example 10
Refer to the data in Example 8 that showed the price of certain item in dollars. The data are reproduced as follows.

5, 8, 10, 7, 10, 14

where, $n = 6$ (the number of observations)

The mean and the standard deviation of the data were calculated in the previous example. Recall that the mean for the data was

$$\bar{x} = \frac{\sum x}{n} = \frac{54}{6} = 9$$

and the standard deviation, $s = 3.1$ dollars (see Example 9 for the calculation of standard deviation). Therefore, the CV:

$$CV = \frac{s}{x} * 100\% = \frac{3.1}{9.0} * 100\% = 34.44\%$$

This tells us that the standard deviation is 34.44 percent of the sample mean. Note that the CV is expressed as a percent, which means it has no unit. Therefore, it is useful to compare the variability of two or more batches of data that are expressed in different units of measurement.

(5) Interquartile Range

IQR is another measure of variation that is calculated by taking the difference between the third quartile (Q_3) and the first quartile (Q_1). Note that the third quartile is the 75th percentile and the first quartile is the 25th percentile. The interquartile range or IQR is given by

$$IQR = Q_3 - Q_1 \tag{6.11}$$

The IQR is the range of the middle 50 percent of the values in the data set. This is a better measure of variability than the simple range because it avoids the extreme values (see the following figure).

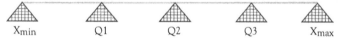

X_{min} $Q1$ $Q2$ $Q3$ X_{max}

Example 11

The data in Table 6.8 shows the monthly income of 20 part-time employees of a company. Find the median, the first quartile, and the third quartile, and the IQR for the income. Table 6.9 shows the sorted values from Table 6.8.

Table 6.10 shows the descriptive statistics for the data in Table 6.8. This table shows the median, first quartile, and the third quartile values. We have explained previously how to obtain these values using the percentile formula.

Table 6.8 *Monthly income*

Monthly income							
2038	1758	1721	1637	2097	2047	2205	1787
2287	1940	2311	2054	2406	1471	1460	1500
2250	1650	2100	1850				

Table 6.9 *Sorted income data*

Sorted data (read row-wise)								
1460	1471	1500	1637	1650	1721	1758	1787	1850
1940	2038	2047	2054	2097	2100	2205	2250	2287
2311	2406							

Table 6.10 *Descriptive statistics of income data using MINITAB*

Calculations using MINITAB						
Variable	N	Mean	Median	TrMean	StDev	SE Mean
Data	20	1928.5	1989.0	1927.9	295.2	66.0
Variable		Minimum	Maximum	Q1	Q3	
Data		1460.0	2406.0	1667.8	2178.8	

Note that the number of observations, $n = 20$.

The median or Q2 (50th percentile) is located at

$$L_p = (n+1)\frac{P}{100} = 21\left(\frac{50}{100}\right) = 10.5$$

This means that the median is located half way between the 10th and 11th value, or the average of the 10th and 11th value in the sorted data. This value is $(1{,}940+2{,}038)/2 = 1{,}989$. Therefore,

Median or Q2=1,989

The first Quartile (Q1) or 25th percentile is located at

$$L_p = (n+1)\frac{P}{100} = 21\left(\frac{25}{100}\right) = 5.25$$

Therefore, Q1 is the 5th value in the sorted data, plus 0.25 times the difference between the 5th and the 6th value, which is

$1{,}650+(.25) (1{,}721-1{,}650)=1{,}667.75$ or,

Q1=1,667.75 or 1,667.8

The 3rd Quartile (Q3) or 75th percentile is located at

$$L_p = (n+1)\frac{P}{100} = 21\left(\frac{75}{100}\right) = 15.75$$

Thus, Q3 is the 15*th* value in the sorted data, plus 0.75 times the difference between the 15*th* and the 16*th* value, which is

2,100+(.75) (2,205–2,100)=2,178.75

Therefore,

Q3=2,178.75 or 2,178.8

The calculated values of the median, Q1, and Q3 are the same as in Table 6.10.

The IQR

$IQR = Q_3 - Q_1$

or, $IQR = 2178.8 - 1667.8 = 511$

Describing Data: A Case

1. *Data*: The data in Table 6.11 shows the compressive strength of a sample of 70 concrete specimens in psi (pounds per square inch). The analysis of this data is presented in the following using the descriptive and numerical methods in MINITAB.
2. *Sort the data. Before conducting any analysis, the data was sorted in increasing order. Table 6.12 shows the sorted data.*
3. *Calculate the statistics based on ordered values.* The statistics based on the ordered values are: minimum, maximum, range, median, quartiles, and IQR. These can be calculated using MINITAB. The values of the selected statistics are shown in Table 6.13.

Table 6.11 Compressive strength of a sample of 70 concrete specimens

Data display: Strength									
3160	3560	3760	3010	2360	3210	2660	3410	3060	4310
3310	2460	2660	3060	2110	2910	3910	4210	4160	3210
3060	3310	3160	4310	3310	3260	3610	3710	2960	3460
2810	3410	3110	3310	3660	3010	3160	3060	3210	2510
2710	3660	3510	3310	3160	3410	3610	3310	3910	3060
3460	3810	2860	3160	3560	3760	3010	2360	3210	2660
3410	3060	4310	3310	3310	3160	2910	2660	3010	3410

Table 6.12 Sorted data

Sorted (read row wise)										
2110	2360	2360	2460	2510	2660	2660	2660	2710	2810	2860
2910	2910	2960	3010	3010	3010	3010	3060	3060	3060	3060
3060	3060	3110	3160	3160	3160	3160	3160	3160	3210	3210
3210	3210	3260	3260	3310	3310	3310	3310	3310	3310	3310
3310	3410	3410	3410	3410	3410	3460	3460	3510	3560	3560
3610	3610	3660	3660	3710	3760	3760	3810	3910	3910	4160
4210	4310	4310	4310							

Table 6.13 Statistics based on the ordered values

Descriptive statistics: Strength								
Variable	N	N*	Mini-mum	Q1	Median	Q3	Maxi-mum	Range	IQR
Strength	70	0	2110.0	3010.0	3235.0	3522.5	4310.0	2200.0	512.5

The positions of the quartiles along with the minimum and maximum values are shown as follows.

Min = 2110   Q1 = 3010   Median = 3235   Q3 = 3522.5   Max = 4310

Note: Q1: First quartile, Q2: Median or Second quartile, Q3: Third quartile, IQR: Interquartile Range=Q3–Q1

From these calculated values, knowledge about the symmetry and skewness can be obtained. Symmetry is a useful concept in the data analysis. For symmetrical data, the "middle" or the average is unambiguously defined. If the data are skewed, another measure (median) should be used to describe the data.

For a symmetrical distribution, the distance between the first quartile, Q1 and the median is same as the distance from the median to the third quartile, Q3. From the calculated value in Table 6.13, we can see that the data is not symmetrical, but is close to symmetry. The distribution can also be checked by plotting a stem-and-leaf, a dot plot, a box plot, or a histogram.

Stem-and-leaf Plot

Much useful information can be obtained easily by constructing a stem-and-leaf plot. The plot was constructed using MINITAB software and is shown in Figure 6.4.

Stem-and-leaf display: Strength		
Stem-and-leaf of strength N = 70		
Leaf unit = 100		
1	2	1
3	2	33
5	2	45
9	2	6667
14	2	88999
31	3	00000000001111111
(14)	3	22222233333333
25	3	4444444555
15	3	6666777
8	3	899
5	4	1
4	4	2333

Figure 6.4 Stem-and-leaf plot for strength data

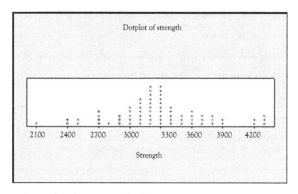

Figure 6.5 Dot plot for strength data

Figure 6.5 shows a dot plot of data. This plot also provides information about the distribution and spread by plotting individual values.

4. *Calculate the statistics based on averages.* The simplest statistic is the average of a set of observations or the mean. In the following we have calculated the graphical summary of the data that shows several statistics including the mean, variance, standard deviation, skewness, kurtosis, and others along with some useful graphs. The graphical summary shown in Figure 6.6 shows the results.

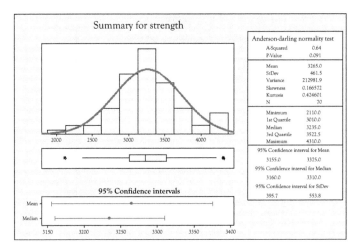

Figure 6.6 *Graphical summary of strength data showing the statistics based on ordered values and averages*

In Figure 6.6, the calculated *statistics based on the averages are shown.*

The statistics based on the averages are mean, standard deviation, variance, skewness, and kurtosis.

The statistics based on the ordered values are the minimum, first quartile (25th percentile), median (50th percentile), third quartile (75th percentile), and the maximum.

An investigation of the skewness (0.166572), and the box plot on the left reveals that the data is slightly right skewed. It is not apparent from the histogram (which shows that the data are approximately symmetrical). For practical purposes, we can conclude that the data are approximately symmetrical. However, the Anderson Darling normality test can be used to test if the data are symmetrical. We test the following hypothesis:

H_0: The data follow a normal distribution.

H_1: The data do not follow a normal distribution

Use the *p*-value (reported under Anderson-Darling Normality Test in Figure 6.6) to test the hypothesis. The calculated *p*-value from Figure 6.6 is 0.091. The decision rule for conducting the test using *p*-value approach is given by

If $p \geq a$, do not reject H_0

If $p < a$, reject H_0

For a given a (5 percent or 0.05 for this case), we find from Figure 6.6 that $p = 0.091 > a = 0.005$ therefore, we do not reject Ho and conclude that the data follow a normal distribution. Note that if you select, $a = 0.10$, the null hypothesis will be rejected. *Interpret the confidence intervals in Figure 6.6.*

Figure 6.6 provides the confidence intervals for the mean, median, and standard deviation. The confidence interval can be calculated for any statistic; and it provides the reliability of our estimate of a parameter. The less wide the confidence interval is, the more precise the estimate.

Confidence interval for the mean

By default, a 95 percent confidence interval for the mean is calculated using the following formula:

$$\bar{x} - t_{n-1,\frac{a}{2}} \frac{s}{\sqrt{n}} \le \mu \le \bar{x} + t_{n-1,\frac{a}{2}} \frac{s}{\sqrt{n}}$$

The previous formula estimates the unknown population mean (μ) with a 95 percent confidence level or probability. The calculated confidence interval in Figure 6.6 is

$$3{,}155 \le \mu \le 3{,}375$$

which indicates that there is a 95 percent probability that the true unknown population mean will fall within the range 3,155 and 3,375 or, there is a 95 percent chance that the true mean is included between 3,155 and 3,375.

Confidence interval for the standard deviation

The confidence interval for the standard deviation is calculated using the following formula

$$\sqrt{\frac{(n-1)s^2}{\chi^2_{(n-1),a/2}}} \le \sigma \le \sqrt{\frac{(n-1)s^2}{\chi^2_{(n-1),1-a/2}}}$$

In the previous equation, s is the sample standard deviation and n is the number of observations. $\chi^2_{(n-1),a/2}$ is in general the $1-a*100$th percentile of the chi-square distribution with n degrees of freedom. In Figure 6.6, a 95 percent confidence interval for the true standard deviation (s) is calculated. This interval is

$$395.7 \leq \sigma \leq 553.8$$

Confidence interval for the median

MINITAB uses non-linear interpolation to calculate the confidence interval for the median. This method provides a good approximation for both symmetrical and non-symmetrical distributions. A 95 percent confidence interval for the median in Figure 6.6 shows values between 3,160 and 3,310. Note that the median is a more reliable measure of central tendency when the data is non-symmetrical.

5. *Determine the appropriate number of class intervals and the width of the classes for this data. Use the information to construct a frequency histogram.* The approximate number of classes or the class intervals can be determined using the following formula

$$k = 1 + 3.33 \log n$$

Where, k=number of class intervals, and n=number of observations. There are n=70 observations in our example, therefore

$$k = 1 + 3.33 \log 70 = 7.144$$

The number of classes should be 7 or 8. The width of each class interval can be determined by

$$\text{Width} = \frac{\text{Maximum} - \text{Minimum}}{\text{No. of Classes}} = \frac{4310 - 2110}{8} = 275$$

A histogram with eight class intervals with a class width of 275 can now be constructed. Note that the aforementioned formulas do not provide exact values for the number of classes and the class width. They provide approximate values.

To construct a histogram with eight class intervals, Excel or Minitab can be used. We used Minitab to construct the histogram. Figure 6.7 shows the resulting histogram.

Figure 6.8 shows that the details in the distribution are lost if too few intervals are used. Similarly, using too many intervals may result into unnecessary details. Therefore, using too few or too many intervals may not display the distribution correctly.

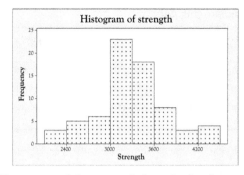

Figure 6.7 Histogram of the strength data (eight class intervals)

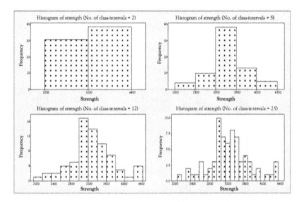

Figure 6.8 Histogram of strength data with different class intervals

Different Statistics Used to Describe the Data

Different statistics used to describe the data are summarized in Table 6.14
    Relationship Between the Mean and Standard Deviation
    There are two important rules that describe the relationship between the mean and standard deviation. These are:

1. Chebyshev's Theorem, and
2. Empirical Rule

Chebyshev's theorem enables us to determine the percent of observations in a data set which are within a specified number of standard deviations from the mean. This rule applies to any shape, symmetrical or skewed whereas, the empirical rule applies to symmetrical data. Both Chebyshev's and empirical rules are discussed in the following.

Table 6.14 Summarizing data

Statistics based on ordered values	Minimum, first quartile, median, third quartile, maximum, interquartile range
Statistics based on averages	Mean, standard deviation, variance, skewness, kurtosis
Describing distributions (symmetrical, bell-shaped or normal)	Mean and standard deviation

Chebyshev's Theorem

This theorem states that *no matter what the shape of the distribution* (symmetrical or skewed):

- At least 75 percent of all observations will fall within ±2 standard deviation of the mean;
- At least 89 percent of the observation will fall within ±3 standard deviation of the mean;
- At least 94 percent of the observations will fall within ±4 standard deviation of the mean.

To understand the aforementioned statements, consider this example. Suppose a sample of 100 students (n=100) were given a statistics test. The average or the mean of the test score was 80 and the standard deviation was 5. Then according to Chebyshev's rule, *at least* 75 students will have a score between 80±2(5) or between 70 and 90; *at least* 89 of those who took the test will have scores between 80±3(5) or 65 and 95; and *at least* 94 of the students will have scores between 80±4(5) or 60 and 100. These percentages are irrespective of the shape of the test score data. The term *"at least"* in the theorem statement makes it very general.

The Chebyshev's theorem states that:

Within k standard deviation of the mean, at least $\left(1 - \dfrac{1}{k^2}\right)$ *percent of the values occur.*

Where, k is given by

$$k = \frac{x - \bar{x}}{s} \, or, k = \frac{x - \mu}{\sigma} \qquad (6.12)$$

In equation (6.12), k determines how far the data value is from the mean, in terms of standard deviation units.

x_i = data values $\bar{x}$ = sample mean

μ = population mean s = sample standard deviation σ = population standard deviation

Empirical Rule

The empirical rule applies to *symmetrical or bell-shaped data* which is commonly known as the *normal distribution*. Unlike the Chebyshev's theorem that applies to any shape (skewed or symmetrical); the empirical rule applies to symmetrical shape. This rule states that if the data are symmetrical or bell-shaped:

Approximately 68 percent of the observations will lie between the mean and ±1 standard deviation or, $\mu \pm 1\sigma$ will contain approximately 68 percent of the observations

Approximately 95 percent of the observations will lie between the mean and ±2 standard deviation or, $\mu \pm 2\sigma$ will contain approximately 95 percent of the observations

Approximately 99.73 percent of the observations will lie between the mean and ±3 standard deviation or, $\mu \pm 3\sigma$ will contain approximately 99.7 percent of the observations

The empirical rule is graphically shown in Figure 6.9.

Example 12

Consider a data set with bell-shaped or symmetrical distribution with mean $\mu = 80$ and standard deviation $\sigma = 5$. Determine the proportion of observations within each of the following ranges:

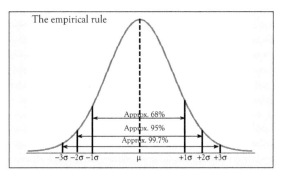

Figure 6.9 Areas under the normal or bell shaped curve

[a] 75 and 85 [b] 70 and 90 [c] 65 and 95.

Solution: Since the data have a bell-shaped or symmetrical distribution, we can apply the empirical rule to find the percent of observation within each of the range.

[a] Note that the range 75 to 85 is within one standard deviation of the mean. That is,

$$\mu \pm 1\sigma = 80 \pm 5 = 75,85$$

From the empirical rule we know that the mean ±1 standard deviation contains approximately 68 percent of the observations. Therefore, approximately 68 percent of the observations will be contained within 75 and 85.

In a similar way, you can determine that approximately 95 percent of the observations lie between 70 and 90; and approximately 99.7 percent of the observations lie between 65 and 95 because the values 70 and 90, and 65 and 95 are between ±2 and 3 standard deviations from the mean.

The previous problem was simple because all the data values were one, two, or three standard deviation units away from the mean. Suppose we want to determine the percentage of observations between 80 and 86 (with the same mean and standard deviation as the previously shown example). From the example above, we know that the value 85 is +1 standard deviation from the mean, so 86 will be slightly higher than 1 standard deviation. To know how far the value 86 is from the mean, we use a formula known as *the z-score formula*. This formula is written as

$$z = \frac{x - \mu}{\sigma} \qquad (6.13)$$

where,

z = distance from the mean to the point of interest in terms of standard deviation unit

x = point of interest,

μ = mean,

σ = standard deviation

Using the previous formula, we can determine how far any value is from the mean in terms of standard deviations. If we want to know the percentage of observations between 80 and 86, we can use the z score formula to determine the z-value (see Figure 6.10).

Applying the z-score formula, we find

$$z = \frac{x - \mu}{\sigma} = \frac{86 - 80}{5} = 1.2$$

It means that the value 86 is 1.2 standard deviations from the mean. According to the empirical rule approximately 68 percent of the observations fall within ±1 standard deviation of the mean. This means that +1 standard deviation will contain approximately half of 68 percent or approximately 34 percent. So what percentage corresponds to Z = +1.2 standard deviation? It must be higher than 34 percent. To know the exact percentage, we need to look into the *Standard Normal Table, or z-table*. This table can be found in the appendix. Using this table, we can find the area or percentage for any z-value.

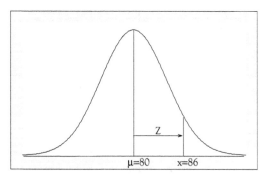

Figure 6.10 Area between 80 and 86

The normal table provides the area or the percentage corresponding to a z values. Note that the z values tell how far a point of interest is from the mean. The z value is stated in terms of standard deviations. For example, the z value calculated using the z-formula for x=86 is 1.2 (as previously shown). Using a normal table, we can read the area or the percentage corresponding to z=1.2. If the z value equals 1, 2, or 3 standard deviations then from the empirical rule we know the percentages. If z is other than 1, 2, or 3 standard deviations, we can find the percentage using the normal table.

The normal curve is symmetrical. This means that the total area of the curve is 100 percent and the line of symmetry divides the curve into two halves where the area of each half is 50 percent. One type of standard normal table provides the area only for the right side of the mean. If z is negative it means that the value or the point of interest x is to the left of the mean. Note that the area corresponding to z = +1.2 and z = −1.2 will have the same percentage on the normal curve. Refer to the previous example. We found that the value 86 is 1.2 (z = 1.2) standard deviations unit from the mean. Referring to the normal table (Table 6.15), the percentage corresponding to z = 1.2 is 0.3849, or 38.49 percent.

Note that Table 6.15 is a partial normal table. To read the percentage corresponding to z = 1.2 standard deviations, locate 1.2 under the z column and read the value in the row z = 1.2 and column 0.00. If the percentage corresponding to z = 1.22 is desired then read the value corresponding to z = 1.2 row and 0.02 column. The value for z = 1.22 is

Table 6.15 Part of standard normal table (z-table)

z	0.00	0.01	0.02	....	0.09
.0					
.1					
.2					
:					
1.0					
1.2	0.3849		0.3888		
:					
3.0	0.4987				0.4990

0.3888 or (38.88 percent). Using this table, the percentage or area for the value of z up to two decimal places can be read. Note that $z = 3.0$ contains 0.4987 or (49.87 percent) of the values. This is because the empirical rule states that ±3 standard deviations contain approximately 99.7 percent of the values, so $z = +3.0$ will contain approximately half or 49.87 percent of the observations.

Standardized Value

The computed z value is also known as the *standardized value of z*. Recall that the z-score or the z-value refers to the number of standard deviations a random value x (or the point of interest, x) is from the mean. This standardized or the z-value is computed using equation (6.13). This formula is used based on the assumption that variable x of interest has a symmetrical normal distribution with mean μ and standard deviation σ. When a random value x is converted to a standardized value z; the standardized value z has a mean $\mu = 0$ and standard deviation $\sigma = 1$. The reason why we want to use the standardized value or the z-value is because this value can be easily used to compare x values from two or more symmetrical distributions with different means and standard deviations. The z-value corresponding to a point of interest x tells us how far the value x is from the mean. If z-values are computed for different x values from other symmetrical distributions these values can be compared easily as the values are standardized. The different point of interests of the x values from the same or different distributions which are not standardized would make the comparison difficult. A detailed discussion on normal probability distributions is presented under continuous distributions where we have discussed how the standardized z value is used to compute the normal probabilities.

Application of the Empirical Rule

Figure 6.11 shows the graphical summary of the diameters (in centimeters) of 50 pipes with specification limits of 3.50±0.05. Using the empirical rule, determine between what two values approximately 95 percent of the measurements lie. We will also find the percentage of measurements falling between the specification limits.

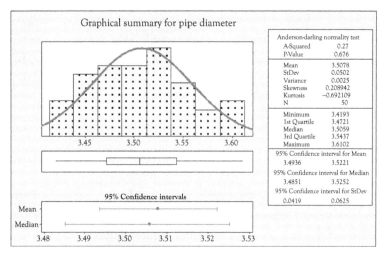

Figure 6.11 Graphical summary of pipe diameter

The graphs and calculated statistics are shown in Figure 6.11. From the graphical summary, we can see that the mean and the median are approximately equal, the skewness is 0.21 and the histogram and the box plot indicate that the shape is nearly symmetrical.

We can conclude the diameter data are bell-shaped and the empirical rule applies. The calculated mean is 3.5078 and the standard deviation is 0.0502 (see Figure 6.11). According to the empirical rule, 95 percent of the measurements should lie between the mean and ±2 standard deviation or, 3.5078±2 (0.0502)=3.4074 and 3.6082. Thus, 95 percent of the observations should lie between 3.4074 and 3.6082.

We found that 48 of the 50 values or 96 percent of the values lie between ±2 standard deviations. This agrees with the empirical rule. We can find the measurements that fall within the specification limits of 3.50±0.05. We found that 30 out of 50 or only 60 percent of the measurements fall between the specification limits.

Exploratory Data Analysis

Exploratory data analysis provides graphical analyses of data using simple charts and graphs. These graphical tools include stem-and-leaf plot and box plot. A stem-and-leaf plot can be used to determine the distribution of a given set of data. We discussed the other applications of the stem-and-leaf plot earlier. Another exploratory data analysis tool is a box plot.

Box Plot

A *box plot* uses a five-number summary as a graphical representation of data. These are:

- The smallest or the minimum data value
- Q1: the first quartile, or 25th percentile
- Q2: the second quartile, or the median or 50th percentile
- Q3: the third quartile, or 75th percentile
- The largest or the maximum data value

In our earlier discussions, we already explained percentiles and quartiles. Calculating these five measures from the data and constructing a box plot are subsequently explained.

Example 13

The utility bill for a sample of 50 customers ($n = 50$) rounded to the nearest dollar was collected. The data were sorted using computer software. Table 6.16 shows the sorted data. Construct a box plot of the utility bill data.

Solution: The descriptive statistics of the data in Table 6.16 was calculated using the MINITAB software. The results are shown in Table 6.17.

Figure 6.12 shows the box plot of the data.

From the box plot, the shape of the data can be determined. In this plot, Q1, Q2, and Q3 are enclosed in a box. Q2 is the median. If Q2 or the median divides the box in approximately two halves, and if the

Table 6.16 Sorted data

82	90	95	96	102	108	109	111	114	116
119	123	127	128	129	130	130	135	137	139
141	143	144	147	148	149	149	150	151	153
154	157	158	163	165	166	167	168	171	172
175	178	183	185	187	191	197	202	206	213

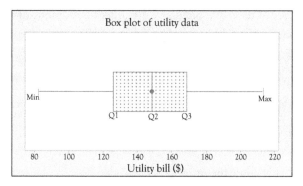

Figure 6.12 Box plot of the utility bill data

distance from the X_{min} to Q1 and Q3 to X_{max} are equal or approximately equal, then the data are symmetrical. In case of right skewed data, the Q2 line will not divide the box into two halves. Instead, it will be closer to Q1 and the distance from Q3 to X_{max} will be greater than the distance from X_{min} to Q1.

In a box plot, the Q1 or 25th percentile is also known as the lower quartile, Q2 or 50th percentile is known as middle quartile, and Q3 or 75th percentile is known as the upper quartile.

Elements of a Box Plot

We will explain the elements of a box plot using Figure 6.13. This box plot is created using the utility bill data in Example 13. The Q1, Q2 (median), and Q3 for this data are shown in Table 6.17.

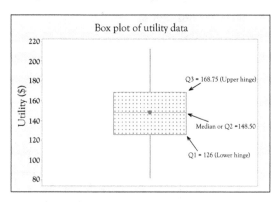

Figure 6.13 A box plot of utility (gas) data

Table 6.17 Descriptive statistics of utility bill data

Descriptive statistics: C1						
Variable	N	Mean	Median	TrMean	StDev	SE Mean
Utility Bill	50	147.06	148.50	146.93	31.69	4.48
Variable		Minimum	Maximum	Q1	Q3	
Utility Bill		82.00	213.00	126.00	168.75	

In a box plot, the quartiles Q1, Q2, and Q3 are enclosed in a box or a rectangle. The top and the bottom sides of the rectangle are called the *upper and the lower hinges* which are drawn at the quartiles Q3 and Q1 (see Figure 6.13). The middle 50 percent of the observations—those between Q1 and Q3—fall inside the box and the difference between the upper and the lower hinge or Q3 and Q1 is known as the *interquartile range (IQR)*. From Figure 6.13,

$$IQR = Q3 - Q1 = 168.75 - 126 = 42.75$$

The median or Q2 is 148.50 (also shown in Figure 6.13).

To construct the "tails" of the box, two sets of limits called *inner fences* and *outer fences* are used neither of which actually appear on the box plot. These fences are located at a distance of 1.5 (IQR) from the hinges. The vertical lines extending from the box are known as *whiskers* (see Figure 6.13). The two whiskers extend to the most extreme observations. The lower whisker extends to the most extreme observation inside the lower inner fence; whereas, the upper whisker extends to the most extreme observation inside the upper inner fence. The lower inner and upper inner fences can be calculated as shown next.

$$\text{Lower inner fence} = \text{Lower hinge} - 1.5 \text{ (IQR)}$$

$$\text{Upper inner fence} = \text{Upper hinge} + 1.5 \text{ (IQR)} \qquad (6.14)$$

The lower and upper inner fences are used to determine the outliers in the data.

Interpreting Box Plots

The IQR is a measure of variability of the data being plotted and is useful in comparing two or more sets of data. The lengths of the whiskers tell us about the distribution of the data. If the lengths of the whiskers are about the same, then the distribution is approximately symmetrical. If the length of one of the whiskers is clearly longer than the other, the distribution of the data is skewed in the direction of the longer whisker.

Outliers: Detecting Outliers Using Box Plots and Z-Scores

The outliers are unusually very large or small observations or measurements relative to the other values in the data set. Sometimes it is important to identify these extreme values in the data as the presence of outliers affects some of the statistics calculated to describe the data. The presence of outliers may be attributable to one or more of the following reasons:

- The error in recording or entering the observed value in the computer.
- The measurement error.
- The measurement coming from a different population.
- An unusually low or high value may occur due to chance.

There are two methods of detecting the outliers:

1. Box plots
2. The z-score

The box plot method is described first, followed by the z-score method.

Detecting Outliers Using a Box Plot

To determine the outliers using a box plot:

1. Calculate the lower and upper inner fences using equation (6.14). Values that are beyond the lower and upper inner fences are potential

outliers. These outliers are extreme values. For symmetrical or bell-shaped data, less than 1 percent of the values are expected to fall outside the inner fences.

2. Define two other imaginary fences known as the outer fences to detect the very extreme measurement. These fences are defined at a distance of 3 interquartile ranges or 3 (IQR) from each end of the box. The observations that fall beyond the outer fence are very extreme measurements and are usually denoted by zeros. These extreme values require special analysis.

3. Denote each of the potential outliers beyond the inner fences by an asterisk (*). An outlier lying beyond the outer fences is represented by a zero ("0"). The symbols to denote outliers may vary depending on the software used.

Example 14

In Example 13, we explained the construction of a box plot using the utility bill of 50 customers. A new sample of 62 customers ($n = 62$) is shown in Table 6.18. The table shows the utility bills rounded to the nearest dollars. Also shown are the sorted values. Construct a box plot of the data. Interpret the plot and determine any outliers.

Solution

The box plots of the data are shown in Figure 6.14.

Table 6.18 Utility bill for a sample of 62 customers

Utility bill ($)																			
82	90	95	96	102	108	109	111	114	116	119	123	127	128	129	130	130	135	137
139	141	143	144	147	148	149	149	150	151	153	154	157	158	163	165	166	167	168
171	172	175	178	183	185	187	191	197	202	206	213	60	45	245	223	256	245	270
280	55	290	302	40														
Utility bill (Sorted- read row-wise)																			
40	45	55	60	82	90	95	96	102	108	109	111	114	116	119	123	127	128	
129	130	130	135	137	139	141	143	144	147	148	149	149	150	151	153	154	157	
158	163	165	166	167	168	171	172	175	178	183	185	187	191	197	202	206	213	
223	245	245	256	270	280	290	302											

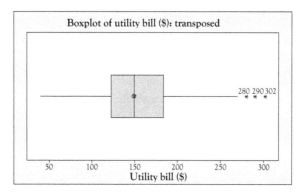

Figure 6.14 Box plots of the utility data

Table 6.19 shows the descriptive statistics of the data including the Q1, median (or Q2) and Q3. The information in this table will be used to perform calculations necessary to calculate the outliers using the following steps.

1. First, calculate the IQR using the information in Table 6.19. The IQR:

    IQR = Q3–Q1 = 183.50 – 122.00 = 61.5

    Note that the Q3 is same as the upper hinge and Q1 is the lower hinge. Therefore, the IQR is the difference between the upper and the lower hinge.

2. Calculate the *inner fences* using the following equations

    Lower inner fence = Lower hinge–1.5 (IQR)=122–1.5(61.5) = 29.75

    Upper inner fence = Upper hinge+1.5

    (IQR) = 183.50+1.5(61.5) = 275.75

Table 6.19 Descriptive statistics of the data in Table 6.18

Descriptive Statistics: Utility Bill ($)								
Variable	N	N*	Mean	SE Mean	StDev	Minimum	Q1	Median
Utility Bill ($)	62	0	155.87	7.21	56.74	40.00	122.00	149.50
Variable	Q3	Maximum						
Utility Bill ($)	183.50	302.00						

3. Check to see if any of the data values are beyond the inner fences. The values beyond the inner fences are potential outliers. Refer to the sorted values in Table 6.18. The smallest value in the data is 40 which is well inside the inner fence. *The values 280, 290, and 302 are beyond the upper inner fence of 275.5. These are the outliers and are indicated using asterisks (*) in the box plot in Figure 6.14.*

4. Calculate the second pair of fences known as the *outer fences* defined at a distance 3 (IQR) from each end of the box. The values that fall beyond the outer fence are highly extreme values and are usually represented by 0s (zeros) on the box plot. For our example:

Lower outer fence=Lower hinge–3.0 (IQR)=122–3.0(61.5)=–62.5
Upper inner fence=Upper hinge+3.0 (IQR)=183.50+3.0(61.5)=368

The sorted values in Table 6.18 shows that none of the values are beyond the outer fences therefore, there are no values that are highly extreme.

Note: The observations falling between the inner and the outer fences are potential outliers or extreme values. Observations falling beyond the outer fences are considered highly extreme values.

Figure 6.15 shows the box plot with lower and upper inner fences, the positions of Q1, median (Q2), Q3, IQR, and outliers. The calculations necessary to detect the outliers were explained in the earlier example.

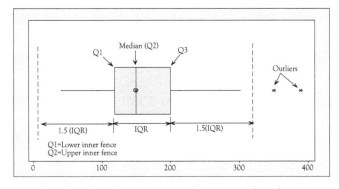

Figure 6.15 A box plot showing main elements and outliers

Detecting Outliers Using Z-Scores

As noted earlier, the outliers are unusually large or unusually small values in the data set. These outliers should be detected and removed from the data before further analysis. One way of detecting the outliers is the box plot. The other method discussed in this section is standardized values of z or the z-score. From the empirical rule we know that for symmetrical or bell-shaped data characterized by the *normal distribution*, approximately 99.73 percent of all observations fall within three standard deviations of the mean. In other words, almost all the observations fall within three standard deviations of mean for bell-shaped distribution.

One way of detecting outliers is to find the values that fall outside of the mean and plus or minus three standard deviations. Thus, the outliers are those values with a z-score less than –3 or greater than +3. Note that the z-score formula is given by

$$z = \frac{x - \mu}{\sigma} \text{ (For a population data) or, } z = \frac{x - \bar{x}}{s} \text{ (For a sample data)}$$

In the previous equations, z is the distance from the mean to the point of interest x in terms of standard deviations; μ and $\bar{x}$ are the population and the sample means respectively; and σ and s are the population and sample standard deviations. Thus, in using the aforementioned equations, the z-score values of less than –3 or greater than +3 are considered potential outliers. Such value should be investigated carefully for data recording error or incorrect measurements before removing them from the data set.

Example 15

The data in Table 6.20 show the price of a sample of 15 flat screen televisions rounded to the nearest dollar. The mean price is \$182.5 with a standard deviation of \$51.6. Calculate the z-score for each observation. Detect any outlier.

Solution

Mean, $\bar{x} = 182.5$ and

Standard deviation, $s = 51.6$

Table 6.20 Price of flat screen TVs

Price of TV ($)									
270	217	131	138	145	161	166	218	95	131
216	219	263	163	207					

The z-score can be calculated using the following formula. We have calculated the z-score for the first value in the data ($x = 270$)

$$z = \frac{x - \bar{x}}{s} = \frac{270 - 182.5}{51.6} = 1.70$$

The z-scores for other values in Table 6.20 were calculated in a similar way. None of the z-scores is below -3 or above $+3$. Therefore, there is no indication of outliers.

Example 16

A random sample of 150 insurance claims submitted to Green Cross health insurance providers showed that the average claim was $1,200 with a standard deviation of $225.

(a) Suppose the distribution of health insurance claim is not known. Can you provide more information to the insurance company other than the mean and standard deviation using Chebyshev's rule?

(b) If the distribution of insurance claims data can be assumed to follow a bell-shaped or symmetrical pattern, what conclusion(s) can you draw about the claims submitted.

Solution:

(a) Recall that Chebyshev's rule applies to any shape (symmetrical or skewed) and the rule provides information regarding the number of observations within a specified number of standard deviations (k) of the mean. In particular, the rule states that:

  • At least 75 percent of the observations lie between the mean and ± 2 standard deviations;

  • And, at least 89 percent of the observations lie between the mean and ± 3 standard deviations.

Applying this rule, for the standard deviation, $k = 2$,

$$\bar{x} - 2s = 1200 - 2(225) = 750$$
$$\bar{x} + 2s = 1200 + 2(225) = 1650$$

We can conclude that *at least* 75 percent of the claims made were between $750 and $1,650 or out of 150 claims, *at least* 113 (or 0.75*150=112.5) of the claims were between $750 and $1,650. Similarly, for $k = 3$

$$\bar{x} - 3s = 1200 - 3(225) = 525$$
$$\bar{x} + 3s = 1200 + 3(225) = 1875$$

This means that at least 89 percent of the 150 claims (0.89 * 150 = 133.5) or at least 134 claims were between $525 and $1,875.

(b) If the distribution of insurance claims can be assumed to be symmetrical, we can apply the empirical rule and draw more definite conclusions regarding the claims made. Recall that the empirical rule states that for the data with a symmetrical shape,

- approximately 68 percent of the observations lie between the mean and ±1 standard deviation, and
- approximately 95 percent of the observations lie between the mean and ±2 standard deviations

Applying the empirical rule to the insurance claim data, we have

$$\bar{x} - s = 1200 - 225 = 975$$
$$\bar{x} + s = 1200 + 225 = 1425$$

Thus, we conclude that approximately 68 percent or 102 (0.68 * 150 = 102) of the claims made were between $975 and $1,425. Similarly,

$$\bar{x} - 2s = 1200 - 2(225) = 750$$
$$\bar{x} + 2s = 1200 + 2(225) = 1650$$

That is, approximately 95 percent or, 0.95 * 150=142.5 or 143 out of 150 claims made were between $750 and $1,650.

Descriptive Statistics Using EXCEL

Most of the numerical measures we have discussed in this chapter can be calculated using EXCEL. In this section, we explain how EXCEL can be used to calculate several measures including the measures of central tendency, measures of variation, measures of position, and measures of shape. In addition, we will also provide the functions that can be used to compute the covariance, and coefficient of correlation.

Using EXCEL Functions

The descriptive statistics measures can be calculated using the built-in EXCEL functions. Table 6.21 explains the numerical measures, their explanation and the EXCEL functions used to calculate them. The use of all these functions is demonstrated using an example.

Table 6.21 Excel functions to calculate descriptive statistics individually

Numerical measure	Explanation	EXCEL function
Mean Sample Mean: $\bar{x}$ Population Mean: μ	The average of observations	=AVERAGE(range) (range is the range of values for which statistic is to be calculated, e.g., A1:A30)
Median (No specific symbols for sample or population data)	Middle value in the sorted data (data sorted from low to high)	=MEDIAN(range)
Mode	The value that occurs most frequently in the data set	=MODE(range)
Percentile	Value such that a specified percentage of observations lie below it	=PERCENTILE(range, pct) Where **pct** is a decimal value between 0 and 1
Quartile	Q1: First quartile or 25th percentile Q2: Second quartile or 50th percentile or the median Q3: Third quartile or 75th percentile	=QUARTILE(range, n) Where n is 1, 2, or 3

(Continued)

Table 6.21 (Continued)

Numerical measure	Explanation	EXCEL function
Interquartile range (IQR)	IQR = Q3–Q1 (the difference between the third and the first quartile)	= QUARTILE(range, 3)– QUARTILE(range, 1)
Minimum	Smallest value	= MIN(range)
Maximum	Largest value	= MAX(range)
Range	Difference between largest and smallest value	= MAX(range)–MIN(range)
Variance S: Sample variance σ^2: Population variance	Measure of variation: it is the average of squared distances from the mean	Sample variance = VAR(range) Population variance = VARP(range)
Standard deviation S: Sample standard deviation σ: Population standard deviation	Measure of variation or measure of deviation from the mean. It is measured in the same unit as the data	Sample standard deviation = STDEV(range) Population standard deviation = STDEVP(range)
Covariance	Measure of association between two quantitative variables. It is affected by units of measurement	= COVAR(range1,range2)
Coefficient of correlation r: Sample correlation ρ: Population correlation	Measure of association between two quantitative variables; not affected by unit of measurement. The value is always between −1 and +1	= CORREL(range1,range2)

Computing Descriptive Statistics Using EXCEL

An example is provided in the following to demonstrate the computation of statistics individually described in Table 6.21.

Steps: As you follow the subsequent steps as shown, refer to the previously shown Table 6.21 for the functions to be typed-in.

1. Enter the data from Table 6.22 in column A of Excel worksheet. The data range will be A1:A21. The statistics will be calculated for this range.

Table 6.22 Home Heating Cost ($)

Home heating cost ($)												
82	145	95	130	102	108	109	111	114	116	119	123	127
128	129	130	130	82	137	139						

2. Type the statistics to be calculated in a blank column such as, column C.
3. Type the function for the statistics to be calculated in the next column such as, column D.
4. As you type the function and hit the enter key, the values will be calculated and stored in the cell where the function was typed.

Figure 6.16 shows the screen shot of the functions as they should be typed-in. Do not forget to type an equal to ('=') sign before typing the function.

Excel's Descriptive Statistics Tool

In the previous section, we explained the functions that Excel uses to compute the numerical measures. These functions are used to compute one measure or one statistic at a time. For example, using the functions in

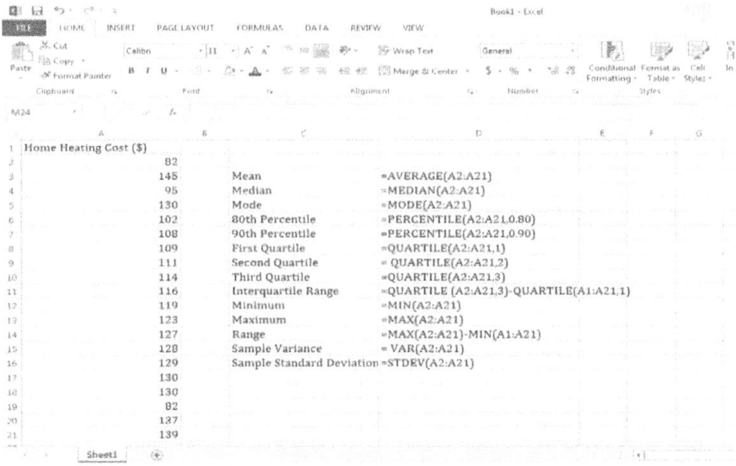

Figure 6.16 Excel functions to calculate the statistics individually

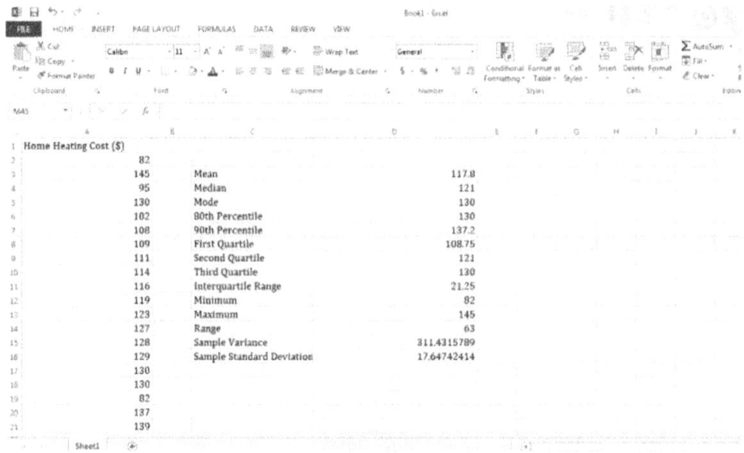

Figure 6.17 *Results of functions entered in Figure 6.16*

Table 6.21, we can compute the mean, median, standard deviation, and so on individually. Excel also provides another option to calculate several statistics at the same time. These are included in the *Descriptive Statistics* option under the *Data Analysis Tools*. The steps to calculate the descriptive statistics are explained next with an example. We will demonstrate how to calculate the descriptive statistics for home heating cost data in Table 6.22. This data was used to calculate the statistics individually in the previous section. The steps are outlined as follows:

1. Label column A of Excel: home heating cost ($) and enter the data in Table 6.22 in the Excel worksheet.
   (Note: You must enter all the data of a variable in a single column. In our example, home heating cost is a variable and it must be entered in a single column for Excel to identify this data as one variable. See the screen shot in Figure 6.16 for the entered data).
2. Select **Data** from the Excel main menu option.
3. Choose **Data Analysis** (extreme right of the menu option).
4. When the Data Analysis dialog box appears:
   Select **Descriptive Statistics** by clicking on it then click **OK**
5. The **Descriptive Statistics** dialog box will be displayed.
   Type **A1:A21** in the **Input Range** box or, click in the Input Range box for the cursor to appear in that box then click in cell A1 and drag

the flashing box down to the last data value in that column to select the range.

6. Check the box **Labels in first row**.

7. Click the circle to the left of **Output Range**.

   TypeC1 in the **Output Range** box. This will identify the column where the results of the calculated descriptive statistics will be stored.

   You may also click the Output Range box for the cursor to appear in the box and then click column

   C1 or any blank column to identify that column as the starting column for the results to be stored.

8. Check the box to the left of **Summary Statistics.**

9. Click **OK**.

The summary statistics will be calculated and stored starting from the column you specified in the output range box. The results are shown in Figure 6.18.

Figure 6.18 Descriptive statistics using Excel

Summary

This chapter discussed the statistical tools of analytics. The chapter provided a number of analytical tools to enable one to master the techniques of describing data using numerical methods, perform analyses and use these methods to compare and draw meaningful conclusions from data. All these techniques use computer software in real world. The following analytics and data analysis tools were discussed with examples: (a) the measures of central tendency—compare the mean, median, and mode, to draw meaningful conclusions from the data. (b) the measures of position—percentiles and quartiles, interpret their meaning, and their applications in data analysis, (c) various measures of variation—range, IQR, variance, standard deviation, and importance of variation in data analysis, The chapter also provided important rules that relate the mean and standard deviation using the Chebyshev's and empirical rule. The importance of empirical rule in data analysis was discussed in detail. The exploratory data analysis including the box plot and its applications were presented. A number of examples and applications of the analytical tools were discussed. The tools in this chapter provide the foundation of analytics.

CHAPTER 7

Wrap-up, Cases, and Notes on Implementation

Overview

The terms analytics, business analytics (BA), and business intelligence (BI) are used interchangeably in the literature and are related to each other. *Analytics* is a more general term and is about analyzing the data using data visualization, and statistical modeling to help companies make effective business decisions. The tools used in analytics, BA, and BI often overlap. The overall analytics process involves descriptive analytics involving processing and analyzing big data, applying statistical techniques (numerical methods of describing data, such as measures of central tendency, measures of variation, etc.), and statistical modeling to describe the data. Analytics also uses predictive analytics methods, such as regression, forecasting, data mining, and prescriptive analytics tools of management science and operations research. All these tools help businesses in making informed business decisions. The analytics tools are also critical in automating and optimizing business processes.

The types of analytics are divided into different categories. According to the Institute of Operations Research and Management Science (INFORMS)—[www.informs.org]—the field of analytics is divided into three broad categories—descriptive, predictive, and prescriptive. We discussed each of the three categories along with the tools used in each one. The tools used in analytics may overlap and the use of one or the other type of analytics depends on the applications. A firm may use only the descriptive analytics tools or a combination of descriptive and predictive analytics depending upon the types of applications, analyses, and decisions they encounter.

Table 7.1 Objective of each of the analytics

Type of analytics	Objectives
Descriptive	Use graphical and numerical methods to describe the data. The tools of descriptive analytics are helpful in understanding the data, identifying the trend or pattern in the data, and making sense from the data contained in the databases of companies
Predictive	Predictive analytics is the application of predictive models that are used to predict future trends
Prescriptive	Prescriptive analytics is concerned with optimal allocation of resources in an organization using a number of operations research, management science, and simulation tools

The term *Business Analytics* involves the modeling and analysis of business data. BA is a powerful and complex field that incorporates wide application areas including descriptive analytics including data visualization, statistical analysis, and modeling; predictive analytics, text and speech analytics, web analytics, decision processes, prescriptive analytics including optimization models, simulations, and much more. Table 7.1 briefly describes the objectives of each of the analytics

Input to Business Analytics, Types of Business Analytics and Their Purpose

The flow chart in Figure 7.1 shows the overall BA process. It shows the inputs to the process that mainly consist of BI reports, business data base, and cloud data repository. The purpose of each of the analytics—descriptive, predictive, and prescriptive and the problems they attempt to address are outlined below the top input row.

For each type of BA, the analyses performed and a brief description of the tools is also presented.

A summary of the tools used in each type of analytics and their objectives is listed in Table 7.2. The table also outlines the questions each of the analytics tries to answer.

The three types of analytics are not independent of each other. The tools used in these overlap and sometimes may be used in combination. Figure 7.2 shows the interdependence of the tools used in analytics.

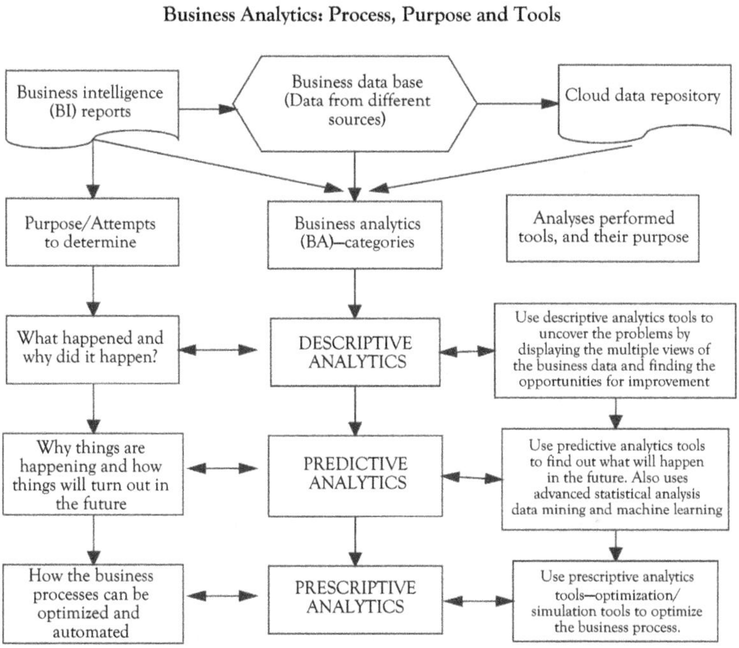

Business Analytics: Process, Purpose and Tools

Figure 7.1 Input to the business analytics process, different types of analytics, and a description of the tools in each type of analytics

Business Intelligence and Business Analytics

BI and BA are sometimes used interchangeably, but there are alternate definitions [59]. One definition contrasts the two, stating that the term BI refers to collecting business data to find information primarily through asking questions, reporting, and online analytical processes (OLAP). BA, on the other hand, uses statistical and quantitative tools for explanatory, predictive, and prescriptive modeling [60].

BI programs can also incorporate forms of analytics, such as data mining, advanced predictive analytics, text mining, statistical analysis, and big data analytics. In many cases advanced analytics projects are conducted and managed by separate teams of data scientists, statisticians, predictive modelers and other skilled analytics professionals, while BI teams oversee more straightforward querying and analysis of business data.

Thus, we can say that the BI is the "descriptive" part of data analysis; whereas, BA means BI plus the predictive and prescriptive elements,

Table 7.2 (a) Descriptive analytics, questions they attempt to answer, and their tools

Analytics	Attempts to answer	Tools
Descriptive	How can we understand the occurrence of certain business phenomenon or outcomes and explain: • Why did something happen? • Will it happen again? • What will happen if we make changes to some of the inputs? • What the data is telling us that we were not able to see before? • Using data, how can we visualize and explore what has been happening and the possible reasons for the occurrence of certain phenomenon	• Concepts of data, types of data, data quality, measurement scales for data • Data visualization tools—graphs and charts along with some newly developed graphical tools such as, bullet graphs, tree maps, and data dashboards. Dashboards are used to display the multiple views of the business data graphically. • Descriptive statistics including the measures of central tendency, measures of position, measures of variation, and measures of shape • Relationship between two variables—the covariance, and correlation coefficient • Other tools of descriptive analytics are helpful in understanding the data, identifying the trend or patterns in the data, and making sense from the data contained in the databases of companies. The understanding of databases, data warehouse, web search and query, and Big Data applications

plus all the visualization tools and extra bits and pieces that make up the way we handle, interpret visualize, and analyze data. Figure 7.3 shows the broad area of BI that comprises of BA, advanced analytics, and data analytics. These topics were discussed in detail in Chapters 1 and 2.

Business Intelligence and Business Analytics: A Comparison

The flow chart in Figure 7.4 compares the BI to BA. The overall objectives and functions of a BI program are outlined. The BI originated from reporting but later emerged as an overall business improvement process that provides the current state of the business. The information

Table 7.2 (b) Predictive analytics, questions they attempt to answer, and their tools

Analytics	Attempts to answer	Tools
Predictive	• How the trends and patterns identified in the data can be used to predict the future business outcome (s)? • How can we identify appropriate prediction models? • How the models can be used in making prediction about how things will turn out in the future—what will happen in the future? • How can we predict the future trends of the key performance indicators using the past data and models and make predictions?	• Regression models including: (a) Simple regression models, (b) Multiple regression models, (c) Non-linear regression models including the quadratic or second-order models, and polynomial regression models, (d) Regression models with indicator or qualitative independent variables, and (e) Regression models with interaction terms or interaction models • Forecasting techniques. Widely used predictive models involve a class of *Time Series Analysis and Forecasting models*. The commonly used forecasting models are regression based models that uses regression analysis to forecast future trend. Other time series forecasting models are simple moving average, moving average with trend, exponential smoothing, exponential smoothing with trend, and forecasting seasonal data • Analysis of variance (ANOVA) and design of experiments techniques • *Data mining* techniques—used to extract useful information from huge amounts of data using predictive analytics, computer algorithms, software, mathematical, and statistical tools • *Prerequisite for predictive modeling*: (a) Probability and probability distributions and their role in decision making, (b) Sampling and inference Procedures, (c) Estimation and confidence intervals, (d) Hypothesis testing/inference procedures for one and two population parameters, and (e) Chi-square and non-parametric tests • *Other tools of predictive analytics*: • Machine learning, artificial intelligence, neural networks, deep learning

Table 7.2 (c) Prescriptive analytics, questions they attempt to answer, and their tools

Predictive	• How can we optimally allocate resources in an organization? • How can the linear, non-linear optimization, and simulation tools can be used for optimal allocation of resources?	A number of operations research and management science tools • Operations management tools derived from management science and industrial engineering including the simulation tools • Linear and non-linear optimization models • Linear programming, integer linear programming, simulation models, decision analysis models, spread-sheet models

Tools used in Descriptive, Predictive, and Prescriptive Analytics

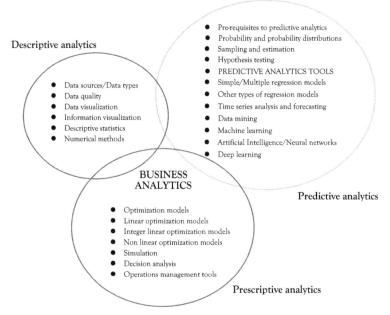

Figure 7.2 Interconnection between the tools of different types of analytics

about what went wrong or what is happening in the business provides opportunities for improvement. BI may be seen as the descriptive part of data analysis but when combined with other areas of analytics—predictive, advanced, and data analytics provides a powerful combination

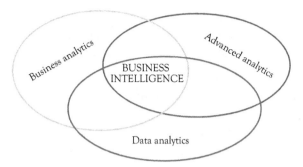

Figure 7.3 The broad area of business intelligence (BI)

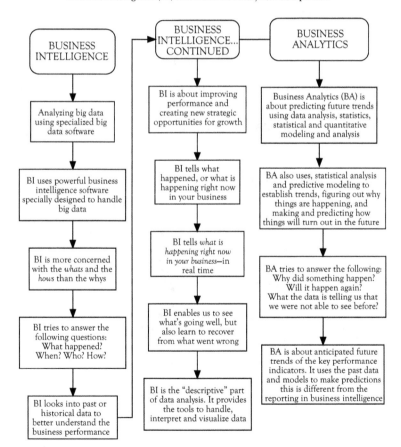

Figure 7.4 Comparing business intelligence (BI) and business analytics

of tools. These tools, as discussed earlier enables the analyst and data scientists to look into the business data, the current state of the business, and make use of predictive, prescriptive, data analytics tools as well as the powerful tools of data mining to guide an organization in business planning, predicting the future outcomes, and make effective data driven decisions.

The flow chart in Figure 7.4 also outlines the purpose of BA program and briefly mentions the tools and the objectives of BA. Different types of analytics and their tools were discussed earlier and are shown in Table 7.2.

The terms BA and BI are used interchangeably and often the tools are combined and referred to as BA or BI program. Figure 7.5 shows the tools of BI and BA. Note that the tools overlap in the two areas. Some of these tools are common to both.

Data Analytics

Another commonly used term in the field of analytics is *data analytics* which fits into the broad area of BI. Data analytics has also been interchangeably used with BA and BI and its purpose is to draw meaningful

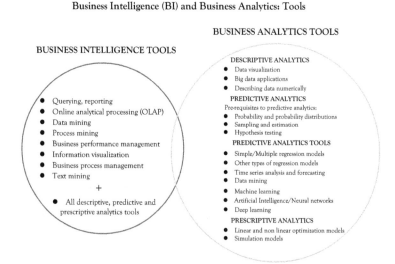

Figure 7.5 Business intelligence (BI) and business analytics (BA) tools

conclusions from the data including *big data* through data analysis. Here, we present a brief explanation of data analytics.

Data Analytics (DA) is about drawing conclusion by examining and analyzing datasets. It uses specialized systems and software. *Data analytics* techniques are widely used in industries to enable organizations to make more-informed data-driven business decisions.

Data analytics is about extracting meaning from raw data using *specialized computer systems* and software that organize, transform, and model the data to draw conclusions and identify patterns. It is all about running the business in a better way and making data-driven informed decisions (not based on the assumption), improving the market share, and profitability. *Today, data analytics is often associated with the analysis of large volumes of data and/or high-velocity data, which presents unique data preparation, handling, and computational challenges. Data analytics professionals have expertise in statistics and statistical modeling, and in using data analysis and big data software. The skilled data analytics professionals are called data scientists.*

Data analytics techniques have wide applications in research, medicine, and other areas listed in the following. The techniques are used to draw inference, and to prove or disprove theories and hypotheses. Some of the areas where analytics techniques are being used are:

Marketing—gaining customer insights, retail solutions, digital marketing, Internet security, manufacturing and supply chain analytics, science and medicine, engineering, risk management, and financial analysis.

Requirements of Data Analytics

Data analytics involves *cleansing*, organizing, presenting, *transforming*, and *modeling data* to gain insight and discover useful information. These are prerequisites to data analytics and are subsequently explained.

One of the most important requirements and criteria of data analytics is *data quality*. The purpose is drawing meaningful conclusions and making data driven decisions. Data analysis has different forms and approaches, and it uses different techniques depending upon the objectives. BI uses data analysis applications that focus on business information.

There are other forms of data analysis techniques with advanced applications. For example, *Data Mining* is also a data analysis technique with an objective of knowledge discovery from large data bases for classification, clustering, and predictive purposes. In statistical applications, data analysis may be viewed as the applications of *descriptive statistics*, *data visualization*, and *exploratory data analysis* (EDA).

Prerequisites to Data Analytics: Data Preparation for Data Analytics

Before the data can be used effectively for analysis, the following some data preparation steps are essential. These are:

1. Data cleansing;
2. Scripting;
3. Data transformation; and
4. Data warehousing.

While data analytics involves preparing data for further analysis, it is closely connected with analytics and BI. When the data is made available using the process described earlier, it is ready for further analysis using the tools of analytics we have discussed in the earlier chapters.

The discussion in this chapter sums up the BA, BI, data analytics processes and provides the similarities, differences among all these methods.

A Business Analytics Case Problem

A case analysis showing different aspects of descriptive analytics is presented here. The case demonstrates the graphical and numerical analyses performed in an online order data base of a retail store and is described as follows.

Case Study: Buying Pattern of Online Customers in a Large Department Store

The data file "Case-Online Orders.xlsx" contains data on 500 customer orders. The data was collected over a period of several days from the customers placing orders online. As the orders are placed, customer information is recorded in the data base. Data on several categorical and numerical values are recorded. The categorical variables shown in the data file are day of the week, time (morning, midday), payment type (credit, debit cards, etc.), region of the country order was placed from, order volume, sale or promotion item, free shipping offer, gender, and customer survey rating. The quantitative variables include order quantity and the dollar value of the order placed or "Total Orders." Table 7.3 shows the part of the data.

The operations manager of the store wants to understand the buying pattern of the customers by summarizing and displaying the data visually and numerically. He believes that using the descriptive analytics tools including the data visualization tools, numerical methods, graphical displays, dashboards, and tables of collected data can be created to gain more insight to the online order process. They will also provide opportunity for improving the process.

The manager hired an intern and gave her the responsibility to prepare a descriptive analytics summary of the customer data using graphical and numerical tools that can help understand the buying pattern of the customers and also help improve the online order process to attract more online customers to the store.

The intern was familiar with one of the tools available in EXCEL—the *Pivot Table/Pivot Chart* that she thought can be used in extracting

Table 7.3 Partial data online orders

				Buying Pattern of Online Customer in a Large Department Store						
Day	Time	PmtType	Region	Order Volum	Order Quantity	Sale/Promot	Free Shipping	Total Order	Gender	Customer Survey Rating
Mon	Morning	Visa	North	High	6	1	yes	194.12	Male	Good
Mon	Morning	Visa	North	Low	2	1	No	40.38	Male	Good
Mon	Morning	Visa	North	High	7	1	Yes	270.87	Female	Fair
Mon	Morning	Visa	North	Medium	4	0	No	186.89	Male	Excellent
Tues	Morning	Visa	North	High	6	0	Yes	279.52	Female	Good
Tues	Morning	Visa	North	High	2	1	yes	220.30	Female	Fair
Tues	Morning	Visa	North	High	7	1	No	279.57	Female	Excellent
Tues	Morning	Visa	North	Medium	5	0	yes	160.70	Male	Poor
Tues	Midday	Visa	North	Medium	4	1	yes	184.96	Male	Good
Tues	Midday	Visa	North	High	8	1	yes	205.39	Male	Good
Wed	Midday	Matercard	North	High	7	1	yes	272.88	Male	Excellent
Mon	Midday	Store Card	North	Medium	5	1	yes	191.83	Male	Excellent
Mon	Midday	Matercard	North	High	7	1	yes	288.94	Male	Excellent
Tues	Midday	Store Card	North	High	3	0	yes	270.75	Male	Fair
Tues	Midday	Matercard	North	High	8	0	yes	275.27	Male	Poor
Wed	Afternoon	Store Card	North	Medium	4	1	yes	174.58	Male	Good
Wed	Afternoon	Matercard	South	Medium	4	0	yes	152.30	Male	Good
Thurs	Afternoon	Store Card	South	Medium	5	1	No	172.39	Male	Fair
Wed	Afternoon	Matercard	South	High	7	1	yes	215.69	Male	Excellent
Wed	Afternoon	Store Card	South	Low	3	0	No	80.89	Male	Excellent
Thurs	Afternoon	Matercard	South	High	8	0	yes	184.19	Male	Good
Fri	Afternoon	Store Card	South	Medium	4	1	yes	181.28	Male	Good
Fri	Afternoon	Matercard	South	Medium	4	1	yes	158.96	Male	Poor
Fri	Afternoon	Store Card	South	Medium	4	1	yes	198.28	Male	Poor

information from a large data base. In this case, the pivot tables can help break the data down by categories so that useful insight can be obtained. For example, this tool can create a table of orders received by the geographical region, or summarize the orders by the day or time of the week. She performed analyses on the data to answer the questions and concerns the manager expressed in the meeting. As a part of the analysis, the following graphs, tables, and numerical analyses were performed.

1. A pivot table, a bar chart and a pie chart of the pivot table providing a summary of *number of orders received on each day* of the week were created to visually see the orders received by the online department on each day. The table and graphs show that the maximum number of orders were received on Saturday and Sunday.

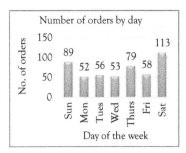

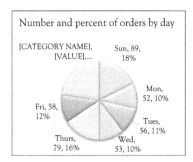

The following table and the chart show the *count of number of orders by the time of the day* (for example: morning, midday, etc.). A bar chart of the pivot table and was created to visually see the orders received online by the time of day. The table and the chart indicates that more orders are placed during night hours.

Row labels	Count of time
Afternoon	112
Evening	65
Late afternoon	20
Midday	92
Morning	33
Night	178
Grand total	500

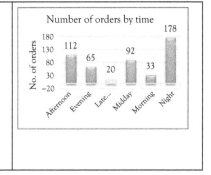

2. *Orders by the region*: the following bar chart and the pie chart summarize the *number of orders by the region*. These plots show that the maximum orders were received from the North and South regions. Marketing efforts are needed to target the other regions.

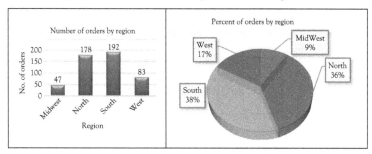

3. A pivot table and a bar graph were created to summarize the customer rating by gender where the row labels show "Gender" and the column labels show the ***count*** of "Customer Survey Ratings" (excellent, good, fair, poor). A bar chart of the count of "Customer Survey Ratings" (excellent, good, fair, poor) on the *y*-axis and gender on the *x*-axis is shown following the table. This information provided the customer opinion and was important to view and improve the process.

Count of customer survey rating	Column labels				
Row labels	Excellent	Fair	Good	Poor	Grand total
Female	25	48	45	38	156
Male	89	62	110	83	344
Grand total	114	110	155	121	500

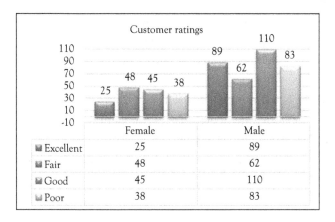

4. The descriptive statistics of the "Total Orders ($)" was calculated and displayed in the table and plot as shown in the following. The statistics show the measures of central tendency and the measures of variation along with other useful statistics of the *total orders.*

Descriptive Statistics: Total Order ($)

Variable	N	N*	Mean	SE Mean	StDev	Minimum	Q1	Median	Q3	Maximum
Total Order ($)	500	0	223.87	3.77	84.23	30.09	167.95	252.62	287.54	371.40

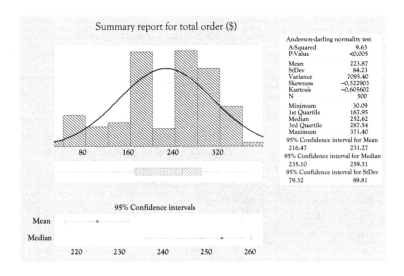

5. From the calculated statistics in part (5) it seems appropriate to conclude that the total orders data is left skewed so that Chebyshev's rule can be applied. This rule applies to any distribution, symmetrical or skewed and combines the mean and standard deviation to provide more insight. This rule is too general and does not provide definite conclusions. More definite conclusions can be drawn using the other widely used rule known as the empirical rule that applies to symmetrical or normal distribution. This rule provides a relationship between the mean and standard deviation of the data and provides

a more definite conclusion. We will show what conclusions can be drawn using this rule in the next section.

6. If the total orders data can be assumed to be approximately symmetrical, what conclusions can we draw about the "Total Orders" received? Use the mean and standard deviation calculated in part (5).

A symmetrical or bell-shaped data that is characterized by normal distribution is often used to draw conclusion by combining the mean and standard deviation. If the data can be approximated by a normal distribution, the empirical rule applies. For our case data, if we can assume that the "Total Orders" data is approximately symmetrical, we can draw the following conclusion relating the mean and the standard deviation of the "Total Orders" data that were calculated in part (5) as shown earlier.

Conclusions Using Empirical Rule: The mean and standard deviation of total orders are:

Variable: **Total Orders ($)**

Mean: $\bar{x} = 223.87$

Standard deviation: $s = 84.23$

Approximately 68% of the orders are between the mean and ± one standard deviation, or, $\bar{x} \pm 1s = (223.87 \pm 1(84.23) = (139.64 - 308.10)$ or between \$139.64 to \$308.10
Approximately 95% of the orders are between the mean and ± two standard deviation, or, $\bar{x} \pm 2s = (223.87 \pm 2(84.23) = (55.41.64 - 392.33)$ or between \$55.41 to \$392.33
Approximately 99.7% of the orders are between the mean and ± three standard deviation, or, $\bar{x} \pm 3s = (223.87 \pm 3(84.23) = (-28.82 - 476.56)$ or between \$0 to \$476.56

7. A dashboard (shown next) provides several views of the online orders data on one plot. The following dashboard shows several plots including order map showing the business activities in different regions of the country, sales by months, percent of orders by time, and total orders by region. The plots are self-explanatory and provide useful information that provide opportunities for improvement.

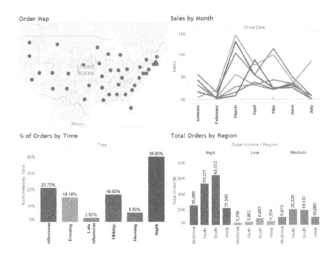

The previous graphical and numerical analyses performed on the online order data provides meaning and insight that is not apparent just by looking into the data. The analyses performed here are some examples of descriptive analytics.

Software Used in This Text

BA is a data driven decision making process that uses data analysis, statistical and quantitative analysis, information technology, management science (mathematical modeling, simulation), and other tools. Often it involves big data analysis. Software programs are almost always used to perform different types of analysis. Unfortunately, no single software can be used for this purpose. In this book, we have used EXCEL®, MINITAB®, and TABLEAU® to demonstrate, model, and perform data analysis. The software applications are not limited to the ones used in this text. Some other software, such as SAS® is a powerful statistical and modeling software that is widely used for data analysis and running statistical applications. This book mainly covers the descriptive analytics topics. The next volume of the book will cover predictive and prescriptive analytics topics. For these, Lingo® software along with a standard statistical software mentioned earlier will be used. The students and practitioners will require training in one or more software of their choice.

Certification in Business Analytics

The demand for BA professionals is increasing. According to recent predictions, the demand for professionals in this area is increasing. This is the age of data and the businesses are driven by data and analytics for current and future business decisions. To be proficient in the use and applications of BA/BI, a good way is to get certified. Many universities and colleges are now offering graduate and undergraduate programs in BA and BI. Many professional organizations are now offering certification exams in this area. One such certifying body is INFORMS. They offer *Certified Analytics Professional* (CAP) certification. Interested readers can go to the following website to learn more about this certification:

www.informs.org/Certification-Continuing-Ed/Analytics-Certification

Another organization offering certification in BA is Project Management Institute (PMI). To learn more about their services and certification, visit:

https://watermarklearning.com/certification/business-analysis-training/

https://pmi.org/certifications/types/business-analysis-pba

They offer PMI professional in business analysis (PMI-PBA)® certification. The certified professionals can demonstrate their skill sets and expertise in the area of business analysis through the certification.

Summary and Overview

This first volume of the book provided an overview of the field of BA and BI. The first two chapters of the book provided a detailed discussion and an introduction to BA, importance of analytics in business decisions, types of BA—descriptive, predictive, and prescriptive and an overview of the tools used in each one. This volume introduced the field of analytics including BA, BI, data analytics, and provided a complete treatment of descriptive analytics applications. It also outlined a list of the tools used in predictive and prescriptive analytics and their functions.

Preview of Volume II of This Book: Business Analytics: A Data Driven Decision Making Approach for Business: Volume II

The second volume of this book is a continuation of this first volume and is entitled:

Business Analytics: A Data Driven Decision Making Approach for Business: Volume II

The focus of the second volume is predictive analytics, its purpose, applications, and the tools used in this analytics. This second volume will cover the following predictive analytics topics:

Brief Content of Volume II

1. *Introduction to Predictive Analytics*
2. *Background and Prerequisites for Predictive Modeling*
3. *Most Widely Used Predictive Analytics Models*
4. *Regression and Correlation Analysis*
5. *Linear and Non-linear Regression*
6. *Regression Models*:
   - Multiple regression models,
   - Non-linear regression models including the quadratic or second-order models, and polynomial regression models
   - Regression models with indicator or qualitative independent variables, and
   - Regression models with interaction terms or interaction models.
7. *Forecasting Techniques:*
   - *Time Series Analysis and Forecasting models.*
   - Commonly used forecasting models
     - Regression based models or associative models
     - Time series forecasting models based on averages
     - Simple moving average, moving average with trend, exponential smoothing, exponential smoothing with trend, and forecasting seasonal data.

8. ***Data Mining***
   - Introduction to Data Mining
   - Techniques used to extract useful information from big data using predictive analytics, computer algorithms, software, mathematical, and statistical tools
   - Types of Information: Association, Classification, Clustering, Sequence
   - Data Mining Applications and Case
9. ***Simulations and their Applications***
   Case on Predictive Analytics
   Introduction to Other Areas Associated with Predictive Analytics
   - Recent Applications and Research Areas
     - Data Mining, Machine Learning, Neural Network, Deep Learning
   - Recent Examples and Applications of Predictive Modeling
     - Some examples and applications of predictive modeling in business, engineering, manufacturing, medicine, signal processing and computer engineering using machine learning, neural networks, and deep learning
10. ***Introduction to Prescriptive Analytics and Tools***

References

The List of Online Research and Related Websites are Provided as Follows

[1] Wikipedia, https://en.wikipedia.org/wiki/Business_intelligence#cite_note-15

[2] Wikipedia, https://en.wikipedia.org/wiki/Predictive_modelling#cite_note-1

[3] Wikipedia, https://en.wikipedia.org/wiki/Machine_learning#cite_note-2

[4] Wikipedia, https://en.wikipedia.org/wiki/Machine_learning#cite_note-3

[5] Wikipedia, https://en.wikipedia.org/wiki/Machine_learning#cite_note-aima-20

[6] Wikipedia, https://en.wikipedia.org/wiki/Reinforcement_learning#cite_note-kaelbling-2

[7] Wikipedia, https://en.wikipedia.org/wiki/Machine_learning#cite_note-bishop-7

[8] Wikipedia, https://en.wikipedia.org/wiki/Machine_learning#cite_note-30

[9] Wikipedia, https://en.wikipedia.org/wiki/Machine_learning#cite_note-1

[10] Wikipedia, https://en.wikipedia.org/wiki/Business_intelligence#cite_note-power-7

[11] Wikipedia, https://en.wikipedia.org/wiki/Business_intelligence#cite_note-8

[12] Wikipedia, https://en.wikipedia.org/wiki/Online_analytical_processing#cite_note-3

[13] Wikipedia, https://en.wikipedia.org/wiki/Analytics#cite_note-1

[14] Wikipedia, https://en.wikipedia.org/wiki/Web_analytics#cite_note-1

[15] Wikipedia, https://en.wikipedia.org/wiki/Web_analytics#cite_note-2

[16] Wikipedia, https://en.wikipedia.org/wiki/Benchmarking#cite_note-3

[17] Wikipedia, https://en.wikipedia.org/wiki/Text_mining#cite_note-:0-1

[18] Wikipedia, https://en.wikipedia.org/wiki/Text_mining#cite_note-2

[19] Wikipedia, https://en.wikipedia.org/wiki/Natural_language#cite_note-john_lyons-1

[20] Wikipedia, https://en.wikipedia.org/wiki/Linguistics#cite_note-1

[21] Wikipedia, https://en.wikipedia.org/wiki/Text_mining#cite_note-4

[22] Wikipedia, https://en.wikipedia.org/wiki/Text_mining#cite_note-5

[23] Wikipedia, https://en.wikipedia.org/wiki/Text_mining#cite_note-breakthroughanalysis1-7

[24] Wikipedia, https://en.wikipedia.org/wiki/Business_intelligence#cite_note-3

[25] Wikipedia, https://en.wikipedia.org/wiki/Business_intelligence#cite_note-21

[26] Wikipedia, https://en.wikipedia.org/wiki/Business_intelligence#cite_note-14

[27] Wikipedia, https://en.wikipedia.org/wiki/Business_intelligence#cite_note-15

[28] Wikipedia, https://en.wikipedia.org/wiki/Business_intelligence#cite_note-power-7

[29] Wikipedia, https://en.wikipedia.org/wiki/Business_intelligence#cite_note-8

[30] Wikipedia, https://en.wikipedia.org/wiki/Data_cleansing#cite_note-1

[31] Wikipedia, https://en.wikipedia.org/wiki/Data_cleansing#cite_note-1

[32] Wikipedia, https://en.wikipedia.org/wiki/Big_data#cite_note-Economist-2

[33] Wikipedia, https://en.wikipedia.org/wiki/Big_data#cite_note-Hilbert BigData2013-61

[34] Wikipedia, https://en.wikipedia.org/wiki/Big_data#cite_note-62

[35] Wikipedia, https://en.wikipedia.org/wiki/Big_data#cite_note-63

[36] Wkipedia, https://en.wikipedia.org/wiki/Big_data#cite_note-55

[37] Wikipedia, https://en.wikipedia.org/wiki/Big_data#cite_note-56

[38] Wikipedia, https://en.wikipedia.org/wiki/Big_data#cite_note-57

[39] Wikipedia, https://en.wikipedia.org/wiki/Big_data#cite_note-McKinsey-41

[40] Wikipedia, https://en.wikipedia.org/wiki/Big_data#cite_note-67

[41] Wikipedia, https://en.wikipedia.org/wiki/Big_data#cite_note-70

[42] Wikipedia, https://en.wikipedia.org/wiki/Big_data#cite_note-71

[43] Wikipedia, https://en.wikipedia.org/wiki/Big_data#cite_note-72

[44] Wikipedia, https://en.wikipedia.org/wiki/Big_data#cite_note-73

[45] Wikipedia, https://en.wikipedia.org/wiki/Big_data#cite_note-74

[46] Wikipedia, https://en.wikipedia.org/wiki/Big_data#cite_note-Economist-2

[47] Wikipedia, https://en.wikipedia.org/wiki/Big_data#cite_note-78

[48] Wikipedia, https://en.wikipedia.org/wiki/Big_data#cite_note-85

[49] Wikipedia, https://en.wikipedia.org/wiki/Big_data#cite_note-86

[50] Wikipedia, https://en.wikipedia.org/wiki/Infographic#cite_note-DN04-1

[51] Wikipedia, https://en.wikipedia.org/wiki/Infographic#cite_note-Ref2-2

[52] Wikipedia, https://en.wikipedia.org/wiki/Infographic#cite_note-Ref3-3

[53] Wikipedia, https://en.wikipedia.org/wiki/Infographic#cite_note-Ref4-4

[54] Wikipedia, https://en.wikipedia.org/wiki/Data_visualization#cite_note-Tufte1983-9

[55] Wikipedia, https://en.wikipedia.org/wiki/Data_visualization#cite_note-11

[56] Wikipedia, https://en.wikipedia.org/wiki/Data_visualization#cite_note-12

[57] Wikipedia, https://en.wikipedia.org/wiki/Data_visualization#cite_note-17

[58] Wikipedia, https://en.wikipedia.org/wiki/Data_visualization#cite_note-18

[59] Wikipedia, https://en.wikipedia.org/wiki/Business_intelligence#cite_note-14

[60] Wikipedia, https://en.wikipedia.org/wiki/Business_intelligence#cite_note-15

Additional Readings

Albright, S.C., and W.L. Winston. 2015. *Business Analytics: Data Analysis and Decision Making*, 5th ed. Boston, MA: Cengage Learning.

Albright, S.C., W.L. Winston, and C.J. Zappe. 2011. *Data Analysis and Decision Making*, 4th ed. Nashville, TN: South Western, Cengage Learning.

Anderson, D.R., D.J. Sweeny, and T.A. William. 2003. *An introduction to Management Science—Quantitative approaches to Decision Making*, 10th ed. Nashville, TN: South Western.

Camm, J., J. Cochran, M. Fry, J. Ohlmann, and D. Anderson. 2015. *Essentials of Business Analytics*, 1st ed. Boston, MA: Cengage Learning.

Eppen, G.D., F.J. Gould, C.P. Schmidt, J.H. Moore, and L.R. 1998. Weatherford. *Introductory Management Science—Decision Making with Spread Sheets*, 5th ed. Upper Saddle River, NJ: Prentice Hall.

Schniederjans, M.J., D.G. Schniederjans, and C.M. Starkey. 2014. *Business Analytics Principles, Concepts, and Applications-What, Why, and How*. Upper Saddle River, NJ: Pearson Education, Inc.

Russell, R.S., and B.W. Taylor. 2014. *Operations and Supply Chain Management*. Hoboken, NJ: Wiley.

Stevenson, W.J. 2015. *Operations Management*. McGraw Hill.

Sahay, A. 2016. *Applied Regression and Modeling—A Computer Integrated Approach*. New York, NY: Business Expert Press.

Sahay, A. 2017a. *Data Visualization, Volume I—Recent Trends and Applications Using Conventional and Big Data*. New York, NY: Business Expert Press.

Sahay, A. 2017b. *Data Visualization, Volume II—Uncovering the Hidden Pattern in Data Using Basic and New Quality Tools*. New York, NY: Business Expert Press.

Stevenson, W.J. 2015. *Operations Management*. New York, NY: McGraw Hill.

Tufte, E.R. 2001. *The Visual Display of Quantitative Information*. Cheshire, CT: Graphics Press.

About the Author

Dr. Amar Sahay is a professor of decision sciences engaged in teaching, research, consulting, and training. He has a BS in production engineering (BIT, India), MS in industrial engineering, and a PhD in mechanical engineering—both from University of Utah, USA. He has taught/teaching at several institutions in Utah including the University of Utah (school of engineering and management), SLCC, Westminster College, and others. Amar is a certified Six Sigma Master Black Belt and has lean manufacturing/lean management certification. Amar has a number of research papers in national and international journals/proceedings to his credit. He is the author of several books including Six Sigma Quality–Concepts and Cases, Statistics & Data Analysis Concepts, Managing and Improving Quality, Applied Regression and Modeling, Data Visualization, and Business Analytics. He is the founder of QMS Global LLC—a company engaged in research, consulting and software applications in data visualization, data analytics, lean six sigma, and manufacturing/service systems analysis. Amar is a senior member of Institute of Industrial & Systems Engineers, a senior member of American Society for Quality, and other professional organizations.

Index

ABPD. *See* Automated business process discovery
Analytics. *See* Business analytics (BA); Descriptive analytics; Web analytics
ANNs. *See* Artificial neural networks
Anomaly detection, 11
Area graph, 114–118
Artificial neural networks (ANNs), 16
Association learning, 11
Automated business process discovery (ABPD), 39

BA. *See* Business analytics
Bar charts, 97–100, 103–105
Benchmarking, 40–41
BI. *See* Business intelligence
Big Data, 25–26, 76
  in businesses, 130
  characteristics, 127
  definition of, 126
  education, 130
  in government, 128
  health care, 129–130
  Internet of things, 130–131
  manufacturing/operations, 129
  in media, 130
  real estate, 131
  science and research, 131–132
  software and applications of, 127–128
Box-plots, 92–95, 150, 179–182
BPM. *See* Business process management
Bubble plot, 121–124
Business analytics (BA)
  application of tools, 20
  applications and implementation, 18–19
  as applied to different areas, 48
  business intelligence, 48–51
  case problem, 204–210
  certification in, 211

definition of, 4
in modern business decision, 4–6
overview of, 3–4
software, 210
tools of, 7–8
types of, 6
Business intelligence (BI)
  advanced analytics tools, 35–36
  applications, 34
  applications in enterprise, 45–47
  business analytics and, 47–51, 198–202
  dashboard, 52–53
  data analysis applications, 34
  definition of, 31–33
  implementation factors, 47
  programs in companies, 45
  support systems and, 31–32
  tools of, 34–35
Business performance management, 40
Business process management (BPM), 36–37
Business reporting, 33, 35

Categorical data, 68
Categorical variables, 100–102
Chebyshev's theorem, 172–173
Class frequency, 84
Closed-end questions, 75
Cluster analysis, 12
Cluster bar chart, 98–99
Clustering technique
  classification *vs.*, 13
  definition of, 12
Coefficient of correlation, 118–120
Coefficient of variation, 162–163
Confidence interval, 169–170
Connected line plot, 113
Continuous data, 69–70
Continuous variable, 70
Cross-sectional data, 68

Data analysis, 42
  current developments, 60–61
  preparation for, 61
  requirements of, 61–62
  using tools, 75–76
Data analytics
  data analysis and, 42–43
  data preparation, 43, 204
  data related terms applied to, 76–77
  definition of, 42, 202–203
  prerequisites to, 43, 204
  requirements of, 43, 203–204
  tools and applications of, 44–45
Data cleaning, 62
Data cleansing, 54, 62
Data collection process, 70
Data elements, 68–69
Data measurement levels, 70
Data measurement scales, 71
Data mining
  analytics tools and, 6
  description of, 5, 77
  machine learning, 14–15
  in predictive analytics, 8
Data point, 68
Data quality, 63–65, 77–78
Data quality assurance (DQA), 64
Data sources, 73–75
Data transformation, 54, 62–63
Data visualization
  area graph, 114–118
  bar charts, 97–100, 103–105
  box-plots, 92–95
  bubble plot, 121–124
  coefficient of correlation, 118–120
  collection and presentation of data, 82
  concepts of, 81–82
  connected line plot, 113
  conventional and simple techniques, 90
  dot plots, 95–97
  forms of, 133
  fundamental concepts in, 132–133
  graphical display of variation, 89–90
  graphical displays, 133–134

graphical summary of data, 87–89
information displays, 136
interval plots, 107–108
organizing data, 83
overview of, 80–81
pie charts, 105–107
quantitative messages, 134–135
scatter plot with regression, 120–121
sequence plot, 110–113
software applications, 136–138
software tools for, 135
stem-and-leaf plot, 90–92
terminology for, 135–136
time series plots, 108–110
visual analytics and, 125–126
Data vs. data quality, 43–44
Data warehouse, 53–54, 77
Data wrangling, 62
Deep learning, 15, 17–18
Descriptive analytics
  aspect of, 7–8
  definition of, 7
  overview of, 55–56
  tools of, 8
Descriptive statistics. See also Statistics
  attempting questions, 198
  using EXCEL, 189–193
Discrete data, 69
Discrete variable, 70
Dot plots, 95–97, 167
DQA. See Data quality assurance

EDW. See Enterprise data warehouse
Empirical rule, 173–174, 177–178
Enterprise data warehouse (EDW), 77
Enterprise reporting, 35
EXCEL functions, 189–193
Exploratory data analysis, 178–179

Forecasting techniques, 9
Frequency distribution
  histogram, 86–87
  summarizing quantitative data, 84–86

Graph, 136
Graphical displays, 133–134

Histogram, 86–87, 170–171

Inferential statistics, 66
Information displays, 136
Information visualization, 136
INFORMS. *See* Institute of
    Operations Research and
    Management Science
Institute of Operations Research
    and Management Science
    (INFORMS), 195
Internet of Things (IOT), 27
Interquartile range (IQR), 149,
    163–165
Interval plot, 107–108
Interval scale, 72
IOT. *See* Internet of Things
IQR. *See* Interquartile range

KDDs. *See* Knowledge discovery in
    databases
Key performance indicators (KPIs),
    53
Knowledge discovery in databases
    (KDDs), 39
KPIs. *See* Key performance
    indicators

Left skewed distribution, 148
Lower class boundary, 84
Lower class limit, 84

Machine learning, 14–16
Mail surveys, 75
Mean
    of data, 141–143
    disadvantages of, 143
    weighted, 144–145
Measures of central tendency, 141
Measures of dispersion, 154–165
Measures of position, 149–154
Measures of variation, 154–165
Median, 145–146
Metrics, 45–46, 53
Mode, 146–148

Negatively skewed distribution, 148
Nominal scale, 71

OLAP. *See* Online analytical
    processing
Online analytical processing (OLAP),
    36
Open-end questions, 75
Operational definition, 75
Ordinal scale, 71
Outliers, 182–188

Parameter, 66
Percentiles, 149–154
Performance measurement, 45–46
Pie charts, 105–107
Population, 66
Population mean, 67
Population parameters, 67
Positively skewed distribution, 148
Predictive analytics
    attempting questions, 199–200
    categories of, 10
    classification, 11
    cluster analysis, 12
    clustering technique, 12
    definition of, 4, 8
    other areas associated with, 13
    tools and applications of, 10–12
    tools for, 9–10
    used models for, 8–9
Predictive modeling, 4
Prescriptive analytics, 17–18
Process mining, 39

Qualitative data, 68
Quantitative data, 68
Quantitative messages, 134–135
Quartiles, 149–154

Range, 156–157
Ratio scale, 72
Raw data, 63
Regression models, variations of, 8–9
Reinforcement learning, 15
Right skewed distribution, 148

Sample, 66
Sample statistics, 67
Scatter plot with regression, 120–121
Scripting, 62

Script language, 62
Sequence plot, 110–113
Stacked bar charts, 99–100
Standard deviation, 161–162
Standardized value, 177
Statistical techniques, 68
Statistics. *See also* Descriptive statistics
    characteristics, 65
    definition of, 60, 65
    statistical methods and, 66–67
Stem-and-leaf plot, 90–92, 166–167
Structured *vs.* unstructured data, 28,
    77
Supervised learning, 15
Symmetrical distribution, 148

Table, 136
Telephone surveys, 75
Text analytics, 41–42
Text mining, 40–41

Time series data, 68
Time series plots, 108–110

Unsupervised learning, 12, 15
Upper class boundary, 84
Upper class limit, 84

Variable, 69
Variance, 157–161
Vertical bar chart, 98
Visual analytics
    data visualization and, 125–126
    description of, 126
Visual objects, 136

Web analytics, 38–39
Weighted mean, 144–145

z-score formula, 174–177

OTHER TITLES IN OUR BIG DATA AND BUSINESS ANALYTICS COLLECTION

Mark Ferguson, University of South Carolina, Editor

- *Business Intelligence and Data Mining* by Anil Maheshwari
- *Data Mining Models* by David L. Olson
- *Big Data War: How to Survive Global Big Data Competition* by Patrick Park
- *Analytics Boot Camp: Basic Analytics for Business Students and Professionals* by Linda Herkenhoff and John Fogli
- *Location Analytics for Business: The Research and Marketing Strategic Advantage* by David Z. Beitz

FORTHCOMING TITLE FOR THIS COLLECTION

- *Predictive Analytics: An Introduction to Big Data, Data Mining, and Text Mining* by Barry Keating

Announcing the Business Expert Press Digital Library

Concise e-books business students need for classroom and research

This book can also be purchased in an e-book collection by your library as

- a one-time purchase,
- that is owned forever,
- allows for simultaneous readers,
- has no restrictions on printing, and
- can be downloaded as PDFs from within the library community.

Our digital library collections are a great solution to beat the rising cost of textbooks. E-books can be loaded into their course management systems or onto students' e-book readers.
The **Business Expert Press** digital libraries are very affordable, with no obligation to buy in future years. For more information, please visit **www.businessexpertpress.com/librarians**. To set up a trial in the United States, please email **sales@businessexpertpress.com**.

CPSIA information can be obtained
at www.ICGtesting.com
Printed in the USA
BVHW091221070121
596911BV00007B/180